“My Mind Set on Freedom”

"MY MIND SET ON FREEDOM"

A History of the Civil Rights Movement, 1954–1968

John A. Salmond

The American Ways Series

IVAN R. DEE *Chicago*

 For information, address: Ivan R. Dee, Inc., 1332 North Halsted Street, Chicago 60622. Manufactured in the United States of America and printed on acid-free paper.

Library of Congress Cataloging-in-Publication Data:
Salmond, John A.
"My mind set on freedom" : a history of the civil rights movement, 1954–1968 / John A. Salmond.
p. cm. — (The American ways series)
Includes bibliographical references and index.
ISBN 1-56663-140-8 (cloth : alk. paper). — ISBN 1-56663-141-6 (pbk. : alk. paper)
1. Civil rights movements—United States—History—20th century. 2. Afro-Americans—Civil rights. 3. United States—Race relations. I. Title. II. Series.
E185.61.S28 1997
973'.0496073—DC20 96-31675

To the memory of my father,
Rev. Dr. James David Salmond

"Hewn from the Rock"

Contents

Preface *ix*

1 The Gathering Storm 3
First legal challenges. The New Deal. Regional protest groups. Local organizations. The Emmett Till case. The Brown decision announced.

2 The Schoolhouse Door 27
Reaction to the Brown decision. Autherine Lucy. Crisis at Little Rock. Massive resistance. James Meredith at Ole Miss. George Wallace and the University of Alabama.

3 "I Have a Dream" 51
The Montgomery Bus Boycott. The rise of Martin Luther King, Jr. King's philosophy. The formation of SCLC. Failure at Albany. The Birmingham campaign. Kennedy's involvement. The March on Washington.

4 "Sitting-in for Justice, Riding for Freedom" 81
The Greensboro movement. The movement spreads. Freedom Rides. Origins of SNCC. The Voting Rights campaign. "Freedom Summer." Malcolm X.

5 The National Response 106
The Eisenhower administration. The election of 1960. Kennedy and civil rights. The Civil Rights Act of 1964. White backlash. The Mississippi Freedom Democratic party. The election of 1964.

6 The End of the Movement 127
The Selma campaign. The Voting Rights Act of 1965. The end of school segregation. Collapse of the movement. "Black power." King's Chicago sojourn. The "Poor People's Campaign." The death of Martin Luther King.

7 The New South 149
Effect of the Voting Rights Act. Black political participation. School desegregation and its effects. Southern justice. The wealth disparity. King's legacy.

A Note on Sources 165

Index 169

Preface

IN THE LATE 1890s a Charleston, South Carolina, newspaper editor, concerned at the escalation of local and state ordinances aimed at keeping white and black Southerners apart, attempted to pour ridicule on racial segregation. His purpose was to make its absurdity obvious to all. "If there must be Jim Crow cars on the railroad," he wrote derisively,

> there should be Jim Crow cars on the street railways. Also on passenger boats. . . . If there are to be Jim Crow cars, moreover, there should be Jim Crow waiting saloons at all stations, and Jim Crow eating houses. There should be Jim Crow sections of the jury box, and a separate Jim Crow dock and witness stand in every court—and a Jim Crow Bible for colored witnesses to kiss. It would be advisable also to have a Jim Crow section in county auditors' and treasurers' offices for the accommodation of colored taxpayers.

The editor was not serious, of course, but simply pointing to the ludicrous situation that current policies would eventually lead to. Yet, as the foremost historian of segregation, C. Vann Woodward, once commented, "What he intended as a *reductio ad absurdum* . . . became in very short time a reality. . . . All the improbable applications of the principle suggested by the editor in derision had been put into practice—down to and including the Jim Crow Bible."

The end of the Civil War left the South devastated economically and psychologically, and with a vast body of new citizens—the former slaves. The immediate response was to create new conditions for this labor force as close as possible to the old ones. Thwarted by the actions of the congressional Republicans, whose moral responsibility toward the freedmen had not quite ended and who also wished to use their votes to create a viable Southern Republican party, most Southern whites were forced to acquiesce as the law guaranteed full citizenship to the freed men and women. Not surprisingly, the former slaves attempted to exercise these rights, initially under the protection of the Union army. By the end of the 1870s, however, the moral impulse had largely departed, and so had the federal troops. Although the situation in the 1880s might have appeared fluid, the direction was clear. Black Southerners found their lives increasingly circumscribed by local and state ordinance, economic pressure, and terror through fire and rope. When during the last decade of the century most states enacted legislation effectively removing blacks' right to vote, their encirclement was complete. As Carl Degler wrote, "The Southern solution to the problem of the races was to be a caste system for blacks in a society dedicated to the proposition that all men are created equal." And what came to be called "Southern custom" constantly found new ways of tightening the noose. Again to quote Vann Woodward, "The Jim Crow laws, unlike feudal laws, did not assign the subordinate group a fixed status in society. They were constantly pushing the Negro farther down."

It would be a mistake to assume that Southern blacks meekly acquiesced in their oppression. They did not. Yet the power ranged against them was such that to confront segregation politically was to invite destruction. Like their slave forebears, they resisted in other ways, including the building of strong institutions within their enclosed communities, particularly their churches, institutions which could be used politically once the national climate had begun to turn in their favor. This little book is the story of how Southern blacks won their freedom.

As always, there are many people and institutions to thank. The School of History at La Trobe University has provided me, for more than twenty-five years, an ideal environment in which to talk, think, and write. My honors students, in particular, have been over the civil rights struggle with me often, yet each year is new. My colleague Bill Breen has, as always, put aside his own work in order to criticize mine, and as a result the book has benefited substantially. Johanna Breen has also given the manuscript valuable scrutiny. Laraine Dumsday has again made sense of my scribblings, and, tolerant of my Luddite refusal to enter the world of computers, has turned them into readable prose. My Head of School, Professor Alan Frost, has been his usual source of encouragement—and the odd small grant. My greatest debt, as ever, is to my family, to my children, their respective partners, and to my grandchildren. The dedication is to my late father, Rev. James D. Salmond, himself a doughty battler for social justice.

J. S.

Melbourne
July 1996

“My Mind Set on Freedom”

1

The Gathering Storm

In July 1946 a young black veteran of World War II, Wilson A. Head, set out to travel from Atlanta, Georgia, to Washington, D.C., by Greyhound bus. Well aware that a United States Supreme Court decision in June had invalidated Southern segregation laws applying to interstate bus travel, he decided to sit where he chose. Throughout the journey he was abused by his white fellow passengers, harassed by the bus company's drivers, and intimidated by local police. In Chapel Hill, North Carolina, Head was taken to the police station and so menaced at gunpoint that he genuinely feared for his life. But he stuck to his principles and eventually completed the journey. The "racial atmosphere" of the nation's capital in 1946 was, as Head well knew, "very Southern in its flavor." Despite this, he confessed to an enormous feeling of relief as the bus crossed the Potomac River.

Unlike the Freedom Riders who later rode the buses in 1961, Wilson Head's journey never made headlines. His was a lone voice of protest, far from television cameras or news reporters. Yet its importance cannot be underestimated. Throughout the South in those postwar years, black men and women like Wilson Head decided no longer to submit to the demeaning restrictions segregation placed on the way they lived their lives. Often for veterans like Head, the incongruity of having recently taken part in a great struggle to cleanse the world of an evil system based on racism, only to find it alive and well on their return home, was too obvious to ignore. Thus, many made their own individual protests, insisting on the right to register to vote, or to use public facilities as they chose. It was dangerous to do so in the South, and some paid with their lives. But the stories of individual acts of courage and defiance, such as the odyssey of Wilson Head, are part of the larger mosaic of America's greatest movement for social change, the ending of segregation in the American South. They are an essential component of its beginning.

So are the stories of a group of remarkable young black lawyers, men who spearheaded the first legal challenges to segregation and injustice, more often than not under the aegis of the National Association for the Advancement of Colored People (NAACP). Of these, perhaps the driving force was a brilliant young graduate of the Harvard Law School, Charles H. Houston. Houston was, in the words of one observer, "the critical figure" who linked "the passion of Frederick Douglass demanding black freedom and of William Du Bois demanding black equality to the undelivered promises of the Constitution of the United States." After a brilliant academic career which left him "the best-educated black American ever to study the law," and a brief period in his father's Washington, D.C., law firm, Houston in 1929 accepted the position of dean of Howard University's law school. Within five years he had transformed the institution. He made it the training arena for a generation of young black lawyers like himself, committed to the notion that blacks must win justice for themselves in the courts of the land and not simply wait for charitable white lawyers to provide it. It was not an easy task: there was money to be raised, faculty to be hired—and fired, and habits of dependence to be eradicated. Yet Houston succeeded. When he left in 1935 to become legal adviser of the NAACP, Howard was unquestionably the best black law school in the country and had already trained young lawyers who were to be in the vanguard of the civil rights struggle, most notably Thurgood Marshall.

Marshall and some of his fellows would in time follow their mentor into the NAACP. There Houston's legal reputation grew, especially after he began arguing cases in court himself. Even before joining the organization full time, he had begun appearing on its behalf. In 1932 the NAACP hired him to defend George Crawford, an African American indicted in Loudon County, Virginia, for the murder of a wealthy white widow. Houston became the first black attorney to set foot in the county courthouse. Although he lost both his challenge to the all-white jury and the trial itself, his very appearance was nevertheless a legal milestone. Jury members agreed that the eloquence of Houston's closing statement had persuaded them to recommend life imprisonment, not the death penalty for the accused—an unprecedented action in such cases in the South.

Houston argued other criminal cases on behalf of the NAACP, but increasingly his efforts and those of his disciples concentrated on breaking down the barriers of segregation, particularly in public education. Houston himself argued one of the first of these cases, *Gaines v. Canada* (Canada was the registrar at the University of Missouri). In July 1935 the NAACP brought suit on behalf of Lloyd Gaines, who had been denied entry to the University of Missouri law school. The university had referred him instead to Lincoln University, Missouri's state-supported black college, which had no law school at the time, or suggested that he apply out of state. Houston argued that Missouri had a duty to provide Gaines with a legal education equal to that of its white students and within the state's boundaries, though he did not expect to convince the court. Nor did he; but two years later the United States Supreme Court proved more receptive. By a 6 to 2 majority the eight sitting justices concurred with Houston's argument that Missouri had to offer its black citizens a legal education of the same standard as that provided for its whites. Given that it had failed to do so, Lloyd Gaines was entitled to enter the University of Missouri law school. It was a judgment on which precedents could be built, and were to be so in the years of struggle ahead.

Thurgood Marshall, too, was making a name for himself in the civil rights area. In 1940 he argued an important case before the United States Circuit Court of Appeals challenging salary inequities between black and white teachers in the Norfolk, Virginia, high schools. He won, thus establishing his reputation as the most able of Houston's Howard group. More important, he established another platform from which the fight to end discrimination could be launched.

Throughout the next decade Marshall's reputation grew as he and the NAACP added to the "chain of cases" they had been building since 1935. One of the most important was the 1948 decision in *McLaurin v. Oklahoma State Regents for Higher Education*. George McLaurin, a sixty-eight-year-old teacher, had been denied entry to the University of Oklahoma's graduate school of education. The NAACP used a little-known legal maneuver to bring the case immediately to the federal district court of appeals, which ruled that the state must provide McLaurin with "the education he seeks." Reluctantly Oklahoma complied, admitting McLaurin to the university but then attempting to segregate him within it. For all his classes he was forced to sit at a special desk in an anteroom; he was kept apart from other students in the library;

and, most humiliating of all, he was not allowed to eat in the cafeteria at the same time as the other students. Back to the court Marshall went, arguing that to treat McLaurin in this way was to mark him with "a badge of inferiority which affects his relationship, both to his fellow students and his professors." In 1950 the Supreme Court agreed with him, and in terms that threw doubt on the whole separate-but-equal formula that had been the basis for the NAACP legal arguments. They had grounded their claims on the contention that the several states had not provided equal educational facilities for their black students, thus they must be admitted to those provided for whites. The opinion in *McLaurin v. Oklahoma* went further.

McLaurin had been given the same educational facilities as whites, no question of that. It was the treatment he had received within those facilities that had become the issue, and this, said the Court, had been discriminatory and must end. The Court stopped short of attacking *Plessy v. Ferguson*, the landmark 1896 ruling that separate facilities were not unconstitutional provided they were equal for both races; nonetheless the justices had given Marshall and his fellows great hope by asserting that equality of treatment had to be real. Moreover, in rendering its decision, and in two analogous cases, *Sweatt v. Painter* and *Henderson v. United States*, the Court had been unanimous. Marshall and his colleagues began to wonder, therefore, if it might be time to change tactics, to stop arguing individual cases of unequal facilities, and instead to force the Supreme Court to confront the legality of segregation itself—in short, to invite it to repeal the *Plessy v. Ferguson* decision of a half-century earlier. In the end Thurgood Marshall decided to seize the day.

Clarendon County, South Carolina, one of the poorest in the state and ruled rigidly by a white minority, seemed scarcely promising ground for a challenge against the very basis of the Southern "way of life." As Judge Waties Waring once commented, the county had "a large population of Negroes most of whom are dreadfully ignorant and poor." Not all were so disadvantaged. The Reverend J. A. DeLaine also lived there, and he was a man of such courage and strength of character that despite hardship and harassment, his determination to secure a decent education for the county's black schoolchildren never wavered, even if it meant asking the courts to declare the county's separate school system unlawful. In DeLaine and his brave copetitioners, Marshall found the means to shift the battleground from graduate and professional schools to the ordinary elementary and high schools of the South and to broaden the means of attack. The target would no longer be the inequality of facilities but segregation itself.

Briggs v. Eliot, as the Clarendon County case was called, began its journey through the court system in 1951. From the beginning, NAACP attorneys attacked segregation itself, introducing evidence from psychologists, sociologists, and anthropologists to show that the very fact of their separation harmed the personalities of black children in a manner that the belated provision of equal facilities could never eradicate. They did not win in the federal district court of Charleston, South Carolina—though one of the three judges who heard the case, J. Waties Waring, did file a vigorous dissent—but Marshall had not expected that. It was the Supreme Court, after all, where the issue would finally be decided.

On its way there *Briggs v. Eliot* was joined by a number of similar cases, all challenging the constitutionality of public school segregation. One such arose from the decision of 1951 of Oliver Brown, a quiet, law-abiding former welder, now a minister, in Topeka, Kansas, to enroll his daughter in one of the city's all-white schools. Refused, he brought suit against the board of education, joined by other parents and supported by the NAACP. This case, too, slowly made its way through the court system. When the Supreme Court finally decided to hear all the similar cases under one label, that honor went to *Brown v. the Board of Education of Topeka, Kansas,* and the self-effacing Mr. Brown had lent his name to history.

There will be much more to say on the outcome of this case. What should be noted now is that a key component in the origins of the civil rights movement is to be found in the work of the NAACP lawyers, trained by Charles Houston and his Howard University colleagues, who by 1954 had had more than two decades' experience in challenging segregation in the nation's courts, building the scaffolding from which the final assault was mounted.

The origins of the civil rights movement can also be found in Franklin Roosevelt's New Deal and in the spirit of change and possibility it engendered. The New Deal never directly challenged Southern segregation, and nor did FDR support key legislation of great importance to African Americans for fear of alienating Southern support in Congress. Yet for many reasons blacks believed that for the first time since Reconstruction they had a president who was concerned for their welfare. African Americans participated in the various New Deal relief programs, though not always on equal terms. The Civilian Conservation Corps, for example, enrolled blacks on a strict population ratio of one in ten, thus ignoring the urgency of their economic need, and kept the work projects segregated. Still, the CCC's companion youth agency, the National Youth Administration, largely due to its liberal Southern director, Aubrey Williams, mounted a steady challenge to prevailing racial mores. As far as possible the NYA enrolled African Americans according to economic need, not population ratio. Williams also tried to establish integrated workplaces, even in the South. He was not always successful, but the very effort helps explain the support blacks gave to the New Deal. At a time of acute economic distress, even imperfect inclusion made a real difference.

The New Deal also gave African Americans a visibility in Washington they had not enjoyed for generations. A few gained senior government posts or were appointed to consultative bodies; others were received by the president or, more frequently, by his wife, or treated with respect in other ways. Tokenism it may have been by the standards of later generations, but to a people who had been largely ignored for decades, even minimal recognition was sufficient to hint at the possibilities for further change.

Despite the essential conservatism of much New Deal legislation, the prevailing climate in 1930s Washington was much more radical, as indeed was the temper of the country. Change was in the air, and in such a climate old attitudes were bound to be questioned, including the Southern caste system. Among those who challenged it were a remarkable group of young white Southerners, drawn to Washington by the attraction of the New Deal, at once proud of their region and acutely conscious of its economic and social deficiencies. A few of them, convinced that racial injustice was at the heart of the South's backwardness, became committed themselves to end it. They worked for a range of New Deal agencies: Aubrey Williams was at the NYA, one of the most liberal of FDR's creations; Clifford Durr, another Alabaman, was a lawyer with the Reconstruction Finance Corporation, scarcely a hotbed of radicalism. A few, like Virginia's Lucy Randolph Mason, were not formally part of the government at all but worked with private agencies closely allied with the New Deal. Together they formed both a Southern social set—sometimes partying at the home of the young Texas congressman Lyndon B. Johnson—and a pressure group for regional change. From 1938 the institution through which many of them worked was the Southern Conference for Human Welfare.

The SCHW was very much a product of the New Deal's reform climate. It provided white Southern liberals a forum within which to work for social and economic change in their region. The active interest of such national figures as Justice Hugo Black, Aubrey Williams, and especially Mrs. Roosevelt, who attended its first meeting in Birmingham, ensured it a voice in the White House. The lusty young Congress of Industrial Organizations (CIO), a union with plans to organize Southern workers, provided essential financial support. Above all, the SCHW brought black and white Southerners together, for its meetings were integrated, as was its executive committee. Although this insistence undoubtedly cost the group members and earned it the hatred of those who resisted proposals for change, its importance lies in that fact. It was the first interracial civil rights body to work in the South since the end of Reconstruction.

The SCHW's initial aims were broad, but increasingly it concentrated on the race issue, for it seemed obvious to members that in segregation lay the roots of Southern economic backwardness and social inequality. Believing that the pursuit of racial and economic justice for poor blacks and whites alike was not mutually exclusive, the SCHW fought to democratize Southern life generally and in particular to end the poll tax, long used to restrict voting rights primarily to the white middle classes. Similarly the "white primary" became a target. In the one-party South, the only election that mattered was the Democratic primary, the choice between the contenders for the Democratic party nomination for local, state, and federal offices. When, during the 1930s, a series of court decisions vested in the party organization control of such primary elections, including who had the right to vote in them, those few African Americans who were on Southern electoral rolls were in danger of effective disfranchisement. Consequently NAACP lawyers extended their activities from the educational arena to securing an end to the white primary, and here the SCHW lent valuable public support, the only Southern organization to do so. Eventually the Supreme Court came to agree with the NAACP. On April 3, 1944, in *Smith v. Allwright,* the white primary was struck down. That spring, even in the Deep South, blacks tried to vote in the various primaries. Most often they were prevented from doing so, but now the law, at least in theory, was on their side—and eventually it would be heeded.

The high hopes of those who founded the Southern Conference for Human Welfare in 1938, and who in 1945 planned to make it the vanguard of a mass movement to bring democracy in all its aspects to the South, were not to be realized. As peace quickly gave way to a new and dangerous type of cold war, and as the country began to fear betrayal from within, the SCHW, which had always had Communist connections, was vulnerable to "red-baiting." It lost its main source of financial support, the CIO, as a result, while its disastrous political decision to back Henry Wallace's Progressive party challenge from the left to President Truman's election in 1948 cost the SCHW the bulk of its liberal membership as its most visible figures—people such as Lucy Mason, Clifford Durr, and Lillian Smith—departed. The SCHW ended its activities in 1948, a shell of its former self. Yet it too, in its uncompromising activism against segregation and its interracial membership, was a harbinger of things to come. Moreover, Wallace's doomed crusade, at least in its Southern aspect, made racism its theme. Speaking only to integrated audiences, Wallace emphasized his determination, if elected, to bring racial justice to the region. Dismal failure as his campaign was, there were nonetheless touches of nobility about it.

Other regional organizations deserve brief mention in the developing story. The Southern Regional Council was one such. Founded in 1944 and based in Atlanta, it attracted business and professional people of both races who genuinely wished to end white supremacy but who found the SCHW's radicalism and uncompromising approach uncongenial. Wary at first of assaulting segregation frontally, it was eventually forced to do so, though its version of an interracial South remained less threatening than that of the SCHW or its successor, the Southern Conference Education Fund.

A few associations were the creation of singular individuals. One such was the Fellowship of Southern Churchmen. The historian Robert F. Martin has described it as a loosely knit interdenominational and interracial association of Christians, "troubled by their regions's mores," who "boldly sought to change them." Under the direction of its activist general secretary, Howard "Buck" Kester, from the mid-1930s FSC members could be found battling on behalf of the South's dispossessed, both white and black. After World War II, with its activities now directed by Nelle Morton in the relatively liberal atmosphere of Chapel Hill, North Carolina, it worked tirelessly for social and racial change through community involvement. Young people like Allard Lowenstein, later a civil rights activist, worked on FSC interracial projects, making contact with local communities. The FSC was "a lonely beginning group," a former member recalled, its members "flag bearers of work for integration and for justice and for peace."

The Southern Tenant Farmers Union was the creation of Kester and H. L. Mitchell, the son of a sharecropper. Centered in Arkansas, the STFU was an attempt through union organization to confront the power structure of the Cotton Belt on behalf of the rural dispossessed, tenants and sharecroppers. By 1938 the STFU had signed up thirty thousand members in seven states, including a substantial number of blacks. As Mitchell came to understand, landlords had traditionally used racial bias to divide those who labored for them. To have any chance of success, sharecroppers had to close that divide. In the end, the power structure proved too powerful and the STFU faded away, but it too provided a brief glimpse of a better future.

Kester, Mitchell, and indeed the majority of the STFU leadership considered themselves to be socialists. Those who led the Alabama Sharecroppers Union had moved further left. The Communist Party of the United States, formed in the wake of the Bolshevik Revolution, was throughout its history the creature of the Soviet Union and its Comintern (the Communist International). American Communists had found their greatest appeal among the immigrant urban working classes and the intellectual elite of the Northeastern industrial cities. Not until 1929 did the party penetrate across the regional divide, and then its attempt to confront the textile power structure in the Loray Mill strike of 1929, in Gastonia, North Carolina, provided it with a convenient myth of struggle, but nothing more. The racism of white textile workers forced the party hierarchy to concede that if it had a Southern future, it was with the black community. In the 1930s, therefore, the party made some inroads among Alabama's black steelworkers and also organized the Sharecroppers Union, a semi-underground, mainly black group, constantly threatened by the local law.

What made the SCU distinctive was that when shot at, its members shot back, most notably in Reeltown in Tallapoosa County, Alabama, in the incident graphically described by

Nate Shaw (Ned Cobb) in *All God's Dangers*. There, in December 1932, SCU members gathered to prevent the eviction of one of their members and exchanged gunfire with the local sheriff and his deputies. When it was over, one union member was dead; two others later died of their wounds, and twenty were rounded up and jailed, to be tried on various charges of assault. Five, including Ned Cobb, were eventually given long prison sentences. To party propagandists, they were all revolutionary heroes. For local farmers, struggling for survival, the picture was not so clear.

The Communist party, through its legal arm, the International Labor Defense, also provided noisy assistance for the Scottsboro boys, Angelo Herndon, and other unjustly accused blacks. It was the motive force behind such organizations as the Southern Negro Youth Congress. It had its organizers in the Southern labor movement, and, most important of all, in the so-called Popular Front period after 1936 it worked on building the alliances with Southern liberals that gained it an initial influence in the SCHW. To this extent, the Communist party, despite its tiny membership, must be counted among the groups from which the civil rights movement grew. Its offshoots, like the Youth Congress or the League of Young Southerners, which John Egerton has described as "a mostly white group of young radicals," provided young Southern activists of both races an outlet for their idealism and a means of working for change and for developing skills which they would continue to use long after the Communist phase of their lives had ended.

Perhaps the best known of these agencies for Southern change was the Highlander Folk School. Highlander was founded in 1932 by two young white idealists of pronounced left-wing views, Myles Horton and Don West. Situated in the Tennessee mountains, its prime purpose was to provide adult education for the Southern working class. West did not remain long, but for Horton, Highlander became a life's passion. Chiefly concerned with the predominantly white laboring poor, and particularly those in the new CIO unions, Highlander did not confront segregation directly—as did the SCHW, for example—until quite late in its existence. Nevertheless the fact that it was an agent for change, that its target was the white power structure and class system, that it trained young people to be labor activists, and that it welcomed blacks to its precincts as guest instructors if not initially as students, was sufficient to brand it as a subversive institution. Horton and most of his staff were charter members of the SCHW, and the link between the two bodies remained close through their twin histories. In time the school placed itself in the forefront of the drive for racial justice. Rosa Parks, for example, whose bold action sparked the Montgomery Bus Boycott, had earlier received training in social activism at Highlander.

Highlander's main focus was the labor movement, and in particular the new CIO. The notion that the American Federation of Labor had shown little interest in white Southern workers, and none at all in blacks, needs correction. Nevertheless it is true that the AFL had generally found the combination of company and state power in the South too tough a nut to crack, even during the first term of Franklin Roosevelt's New Deal. Despite the claim that "the President wants you to join a union," management had little difficulty beating back the United Textile Workers in the 1934 textile strike, the biggest industry-wide stoppage in American history. Toward the end of the decade, however, under the aegis of the breakaway CIO, a new and sustained attempt was made to organize the South's key industries, particularly its textile workers. In March 1937 the CIO created the Textile Workers Organizing Committee to spearhead the drive. The going was slow, and though organizers achieved some success in other, less critical industries like tobacco or mining, by the end of 1939 there was little to show for two years of effort in the textile mills.

Some gains were made during the war years, when management, hungry for government contracts and labor, and desperate to avoid costly work stoppages, was more inclined to obey the provisions of the Wagner Act and the Fair Employment Practices Commission. Again, most of these breakthroughs occurred in industries other than textiles, and often resulted in vigorous recruiting among African-American workers and the formation of some biracial local unions. The success rate was by no means overwhelming, but by 1945 some unions in the South were both taking the demands of their black constituents seriously and attempting to moderate the racism of their white membership. Regional leaders like Lucy Randolph Mason and Paul Christopher were active in the SCHW, connecting the CIO to the first stirrings of a postwar mood for racial change.

The South was marked as the CIO's main recruiting target in the immediate postwar years. "Operation Dixie," it was hoped, would protect and extend wartime gains, raise the living standards of Southern workers, both black and white, finally crack the region's most important industry, textiles, and by implication transform its political culture. It failed to do so, again largely because it could not make significant inroads into textiles, where the bulk of its effort was concentrated. Moreover, while the Southern Organizing Committee leadership stressed that there would be no neglect of potential black recruits, "because they are God's human beings and are workers," concentration on textiles, given the overwhelmingly white mill workforce, meant that the linkage between labor and civil rights activity had to be downplayed. Operation Dixie paid little attention to industries such as lumber, pulp and paper, tobacco, and food processing, where large numbers of blacks worked, where unionism had already taken hold, and where some biracial locals had already been formed. To that extent the drive missed its opportunity and compromised its aims. Nevertheless it had some effect on the caste system, achieved some isolated victories, and made some linkages, at least at the local level, between industrial unionism and civil rights, to which African-American workers could respond.

What of the South's politicians? Was the region's political power structure remotely responsive either to changing regional demography or to the voices of those of its citizens seeking an extension of their rights? As World War II gave way to peace and normality returned, some saw real signs of hope. One reason was the increase in black political participation, partly the result of the ending of the white primary but also flowing from wartime population shifts. Rural blacks, like their white neighbors, flocked to the cities during the war to work in shipyards and factories. There they found it much easier and much less dangerous to form associations, even to express themselves politically. In the South in 1940 only about 2 percent of those blacks eligible to do so had registered to vote. By 1947 this figure had reached 12 percent; it would climb further in the decade ahead. Some Southern local politicians immediately responded, forming mutually beneficial if informal alliances with local black leaders. Easily the most effective was William B. Hartsfield, mayor of Atlanta between 1936 and 1961, who consistently traded votes for services with the city's black politicians. But there were others. Even as unreconstructed a city as Montgomery, Alabama, experienced a surge of black political activity in the postwar years, forcing a response from the local power structure. Black political activity in the postwar South was an urban matter, but, given that blacks continued to move to the cities in increasing numbers, it pointed the way to the future.

Black voters were less successful in influencing postwar politics at the state level, though again there were initial signs for optimism. A new, younger cadre of politicians sought and often gained power in Southern states, men like Ellis Arnall in Georgia, Claude Pepper in Florida, Estes Kefauver in Tennessee, and Alabama's trio of Lister Hill, John Sparkman, and, archetypically, James M. Folsom. These were men less inclined to favor the rhetoric of white supremacy than to talk about the promise of a more democratic future. By no means advocates of integration (for that would have meant political oblivion), they nevertheless talked about enlarging economic opportunity and the quality of life for all Southerners, black and white. As Folsom argued in 1946, "As long as Negroes are held down by deprivation and lack of opportunity," other poor people would be held down alongside them. Willing recipients of black votes, these new political leaders offered some prospect of achieving racial change through regional political action.

So too, on a national level, did the government. Harry S Truman had never been thought of as a racial liberal, and most blacks in 1944 had opposed his vice-presidential nomination. It came as a surprise, therefore, when, scarcely a year after succeeding Roosevelt, in the wake of a welter of racist violence in the South, he appointed the first Presidential Committee on Civil Rights. Its task was to prepare recommendations to secure racial justice in the region. The committee's 1947 report, *To Secure These Rights*, was a sweeping indictment of the South's racial order. Its recommendations comprised a bold blueprint for racial change: a federal antilynching law, the abolition of the poll tax, an end to segregation on interstate transportation and in the nation's capital, the withdrawal of federal funds from institutions practicing segregation, and the establishment of a permanent civil rights section within the Department of Justice. Not only did President Truman endorse the report, he incorporated the bulk of its recommendations into the first civil rights legislative package sent to Congress since Reconstruction. Of course it had no chance of passage, for its main political impact was to so alienate sections of the Southern wing of the Democratic party that in 1948 they mounted a "Dixiecrat" challenge to the president's election. Perhaps Truman's reasons for backing civil rights were narrowly political, given the importance of the Northern black vote in securing his election. Nevertheless his support for the package, together with his executive orders ending segregation in the armed forces and prohibiting discrimination in federal employment, made him the first president in eighty years to move specifically against racial injustice. He both generated hope among African Americans and provided a legislative blueprint for the future.

African Americans, too, working in their local communities and through their own institutions, helped to create a climate for change, something that historians have only recently come to appreciate. Nowhere was their task more difficult than in the South's most rural and racist state. Yet as the historian John Dittmer had shown, the spirit of resistance was stirring even in Mississippi. Brave men like Medgar Evers, often recently returned from European battlefields, were determined to exercise their rights, in particular the right to vote. White resistance was ferocious, the prospect of death or injury ever-present, the law indifferent or actively hostile. The blacks kept at it. Denied access to the polls, they complained to state and federal authorities, usually fruitlessly and at great personal risk in a state where white supremacy determined all. Mississippi was, wrote V. O. Key, "the last vestige of a dead and despairing civilization," a region where as late as 1944, in Amite County, a black minister, the Reverend Isaac Simmons, could be brutally lynched, not for any crime, real or imagined, not even for political activity, but simply because he owned land and had thus excited the envy of his white neighbors. His murderers, predictably, escaped justice.

Yet even in Mississippi local people began working for change. The NAACP quietly expanded its presence in the state between 1946 and 1954, and then became increasingly visible. It openly supported the rights of blacks to vote and encouraged them to register; protested the manifest inequalities in the state's educational system; supported Medgar Evers in his unsuccessful bid in January 1954 to enroll in the University of Mississippi; and in May of that year publicly hailed the *Brown* decision as a watershed in the history of Southern race relations. Much of the drive for this increased activity was provided by war veterans, like Evers or Aaron Henry, who determined that they would no longer live as their parents had.

What was true of Mississippi was true of the region generally. Despite an increasingly intolerant regional climate, blacks throughout the South formed new local NAACP branches or joined existing ones, voted where they could, or protested their inability to do so, more often taking their grievances to the courts. George Elmore was one. A black merchant in Columbia, South Carolina, in 1947 he sued the election officials who had denied him the right to vote in the 1946 Democratic primary. He won his case, mainly because he appeared before J. Waties Waring, one of the few judges on Southern benches not blinded by white supremacist notions. Throughout the region, other blacks were mobilizing for a better future—in the NAACP, in new groups like Mississippi's Regional Council of Negro Leadership (RCNL), occasionally in partnership with white veterans as in the GI Non-Partisan League of Athens, Tennessee, sometimes under the leadership of a new, more practical breed of black clergy, who saw in church militancy a means to social equality as well as spiritual regeneration.

They did so in the face of an increasing tide of white violence and reaction, increased Klan activity, and random brutality and murder. Isaac Woodward, a returning veteran, was blinded in South Carolina in 1945 by local police for no apparent reason. In 1946 another veteran, Maceo Snipes, was murdered in Butler, Georgia, after registering to vote. Mayhem swept the region, often with black veterans the victims, as whites feared they were the vanguard of a revolutionary force aimed at breaking up the caste system. In a way, that is exactly what men like Medgar Evers and Aaron Henry had become. Their examples as men and women of courage cannot be underestimated.

Still, one did not need to have fought abroad to be brave at home. Perhaps the man who best symbolized this determination to be free of fear was an old black farmer from Money, Mississippi, named Mose Wright. In August 1954 Wright's grand-nephew, a stocky, street-smart Chicago boy named Emmett Till, came down for a visit. Till liked boasting to the local fellows, in particular about his success with white Chicago girls. Some of the Money lads eventually dared him to try his luck with Carolyn Bryant, a young white married woman who worked in a local store. Nobody knows exactly what happened, but it seems Till, blissfully ignorant of the folkways of rural Mississippi, went into the store, may have touched Carolyn's hand, asked her for a date—and whistled at her. Certainly he said, "Bye, baby," as he left. Several witnesses, including his cousin, heard that. Quickly his friends, sensing danger, took the bewildered lad back to Mose Wright's farmhouse.

Danger came three days later in the form of Carolyn's husband Roy and his half-brother, J. W. Milam. At midnight on August 28 they arrived at Wright's farm and abducted the young Till. Three days later his body was found in the Tallahatchie River, horribly mutilated and tied to a cotton gin fan. Milam and Bryant were quickly arrested and charged with murder.

Their trial must be taken as one of the symbolic energizing events of the entire civil rights movement for three reasons. First, it received national attention of a sort not normally accorded Southern race murders. More than a hundred newspaper and television reporters descended on Money. Their descriptions of the mutilated body, the stereotypical Sheriff Strider, and the quiescent all-male, all-white jury outraged the nation, as did the inevitable verdict of not guilty. Southern justice and the whole Southern way of life was brought under the national microscope as it had rarely been before. Second, Mose Wright appeared in the witness box, calm, seemingly unafraid, and identified his nephew's killers. His bravery in so doing provided the civil rights movement with one of its most potent symbols. Third, the Till murder had a long-term impact no one could possibly have foreseen. A generation of black teenagers, as Anne Moody later pointed out, recognized themselves in his bloated and mutilated body. Moody, Joyce and Dorie Ladner, Sam Block, and many others who felt similarly about the murder all became civil rights activists a decade later. As Amzie Moore, himself a veteran of the movement, later observed, the Till murder marked the beginning of Mississippi's modern civil rights era.

As the seeds of black protest were being planted in the South, a more sophisticated legal struggle continued at the United States Supreme Court. In December 1952 the Court began hearing arguments in *Brown v. Board of Education*, the rubric for five desegregation cases. Both sides realized the climactic nature of the contest, and their lawyers had prepared accordingly. South Carolina hired John W. Davis, "the most accomplished and admired appellate lawyer in America," and a former Democratic presidential candidate, while for the NAACP Thurgood Marshall and his staff had developed their arguments and had practiced their delivery, often before an appreciative audience of Howard Law School students. The courtroom was packed to hear the three days of testimony, then for the first half of 1953 the justices deliberated behind closed doors. Just before adjourning for the summer they announced a further postponement of any decision, calling instead for more oral argument in the fall. Then came a bombshell. When the chief justice, Fred M. Vinson, died of a heart attack, in return for campaign support the new president, Dwight D. Eisenhower, named California's third-term governor, Earl Warren, as new chief justice. Warren had proved a popular executive, but he had no judicial experience. Nevertheless in appointing him the president had unwittingly made his most important contribution to America's civil rights story.

As the contending lawyers reassembled in the fall of 1953, the NAACP added two historians to its team. The task of John Hope Franklin and C. Vann Woodward was to instruct the justices on the historical context of segregation, explaining that this was no immutable Southern folkway but that it arose from a specific set of post–Civil War circumstances. In shifting their argument from inequality of treatment, as prohibited in the *Plessy v. Ferguson* judgment of 1896, to the contention that segregation was inherently unequal, the NAACP lawyers knew the risks they were taking. If the Court accepted the views of Davis and his team, based as they were on legal precedent, and rejected the notion that sociological or historical perspectives had any currency in a court of law, then the cause of equal justice would be set back at least a generation. When Warren brought the session to a close in December 1953, the issue was still very much in doubt. Both sides hoped to gain a majority in the expected split decision.

Not until May 17, 1954, were doubts resolved. In his first major judicial opinion, Warren announced to a silent, intense crowd of clerks, lawyers, and reporters a unanimous decision that in the field of public education the doctrine of "separate but equal has no place. Separate educational facilities are inherently unequal." Unanimity had not been easy to come by. On assuming his duties, Warren had found that four justices were ready to overturn *Plessy v. Ferguson* and find for the plaintiffs. Add his own vote to theirs, and the decision was never in doubt. But in deciding an issue of such moment, Warren believed, a bare majority was surely not enough. To have any chance of attaining the national support necessary to secure compliance, a unanimous vote was essential. Patiently Warren set about resolving the doubts of the remaining four. By May he had convinced three of them. Only Stanley Reed, a seventy-year-old Kentuckian and Roosevelt appointee, remained unconvinced. Warren talked with him often but never pressured him, for he knew that what concerned Reed most was not the correctness of the decision but how the South would react to it. Eventually Reed decided to go along, but not until the very last moment.

Some scholars argue that the importance of the *Brown* decision has been exaggerated, that change was coming in the South anyway, and, indeed, that *Brown* may even have retarded progress, given the vehemence of the reaction against it. Yet after *Brown*, nothing could ever be the same. Its implications, its very language, went far beyond the realm of public education, crucial as that was. It was a dual symbol. For blacks it was a sure sign that the federal government had finally come down on the side of racial justice. For many whites it was an urgent call to arms and a challenge to their way of life which had to be met. Over the next decade the battle was fought not only in the South's schools and courts but in its stores and its streets. In the end the South was transformed, but at far greater cost than could have been foreseen that bright May Monday.

2

The Schoolhouse Door

THAT THE JUSTICES HAD TURNED the Constitution into "a mere scrap of paper" was Georgia Governor Herman Talmadge's oft-quoted outburst upon hearing of the Court's decision. They had, he thundered, "blatantly ignored all law and precedent and usurped from Congress and the people the power to amend the Constitution, and from the Congress the authority to make the laws of the land." Mississippi's Senator James O. Eastland promised defiance and warned that any effort to enforce the decision would bring on "great strife and turmoil." Senator Harry Byrd of Virginia deplored the "serious blow" aimed at the South's most vital interests, and also predicted dissension and defiance. Throughout the South ordinary citizens echoed the words of their political leaders as they prepared to defend white supremacy.

Yet it is clear that in those crucial first weeks after the *Brown* decision the white South did not speak with one fierce voice of defiance. A number of political and social leaders counseled compliance, or at least moderation, and they too had their constituency. "When the Supreme Court speaks, that's the law," said Alabama's Governor James E. Folsom, making it clear that he expected Alabamians to obey it. Three of the region's most influential newspaper editors, Ralph

McGill of the *Atlanta Constitution*, Hodding Carter of the *Greenville* (Mississippi) *Delta Democrat-Times*, and Jonathan Daniels of the *Raleigh News and Observer*, while recognizing the unpopularity of the decision, all urged acceptance, arguing that the law must be obeyed. Daniels wrote that he expected the *Brown* decision "will be met in the South with the good sense and the good will of the people of both races in a manner which will serve the children and honor America." Few predictions have fallen wider of their marks. Even in Mississippi, voices of moderation could still be heard. Eastland's Senate colleague, John Stennis, warned people to be calm, reminding them that they had years ahead in which to discuss the decision's implications. The governor, Hugh L. White, in an unprecedented move, even arranged a meeting with the state's black leaders to consider his plan to pump millions of dollars into improving black education in return for their endorsement of a voluntary segregation plan. Meanwhile, in scores of local communities, in anticipation of the Supreme Court's promised implementation plan, ordinary folk started planning their moves, and not always in the language of resistance. Aubrey Williams, Jr., recalled how, in at least one Montgomery school district, parents consulted him on how to integrate their school with the least possible disruption. Those who saw in those first months the prospect of eventual general compliance with the decision had at least some grounds for optimism.

As for the South's black communities, the general mood was one of euphoria. Educational leaders, convinced the decisive battle was won, lobbied state legislators for swift implementation, the more so as a few border states, plus the District of Columbia, had begun the voluntary desegregation of their school systems. Louisville, Kentucky, was the most impressive, completing the process in a single semester. St. Louis planned to do it in two. In West Virginia twenty-five counties desegregated, and there was similar movement in Texas, Arkansas, and Maryland, where the Baltimore school system became nonracial during the 1954–1955 school year. Throughout the South, Catholic schools also moved to obey the law. All over the region, blacks responded to the optimistic mood by flocking to join the NAACP. State and local secretaries reported large-scale membership boosts. It was, said John Dittmer, "an exhilarating time for NAACP activists"—even in Mississippi. By the end of 1954 the number of state branches had increased from twenty-one to thirty-four. The bulk of the new members were ordinary working-class blacks. The NAACP took advantage of the hopes raised by the decision at last to broaden its membership base.

One crucial event did not occur in the months after May 17: President Eisenhower's ringing endorsement of the *Brown* decision and his insistence that it be immediately complied with. Had he taken that step, the history of the next ten years might have been much less traumatic. Although he never said so publicly, Eisenhower told enough people privately that he deplored the Court decision, and that he considered the appointment of Earl Warren the worst mistake of his presidency, to cause one to wonder whether he could have made such a declaration seem convincing. Still, he should have tried. *Brown* was now the law of the land, and it was Eisenhower's job to ensure that it was carried out. The presidency carries with it enormous moral authority; add to it Eisenhower's great personal popularity, and his failure to speak out is an indictment of his leadership. "If Mr. Eisenhower had come through," said Warren Court Justice Tom Clark, "it would have changed things a lot."

Eisenhower's failure to support the Court soon gave heart to those Southerners most disposed to defiance. In the absence of decisive federal leadership, Southern whites who advocated compliance with the law of the land steadily lost influence to those who saw political capital in defying it. Journalists, business leaders, and above all, local politicians moved to circumvent compliance by any means possible. Unlike the racists from earlier in the century, they did not immediately appeal to violence. Rather their main weapon was also that of their opponents, the courts. Increasingly, those opposed to *Brown* took to the friendly atmosphere of the state court system for the purpose of litigating obstruction and, as James J. Kilpatrick, the Richmond editor, said, "take lawful advantage of the law's delays." By mid-1955 the law's evaders had clearly gained the upper hand throughout the South, even in such supposedly moderate states as Virginia and North Carolina.

More sinister than those who would use one jurisdiction to evade the rulings of another were those who saw in economic pressure the most effective means of preventing compliance. These were usually, as historian David Goldfield has pointed out, the South's "merchants, bankers, farmers and politicians," the men who controlled "the economic and political life" of the South's small towns and even its cities. Their organization was the White Citizens Council movement. By 1956 local councils had sprung up throughout the region, taken control of local government in many areas, developed a mass base through the clever staging of anti-integration rallies, and though strenuously shunning the use of violence, constantly, through their public rhetoric, reinforced it as a possibility. Economic pressure was, however, the WCC's chief weapon. Blacks who sought to implement the *Brown* decision quickly found their credit cut off, their employment threatened, their very livelihood put at risk in a score of different ways. The pressure was intense, unrelenting, and very effective. Most blacks had neither the economic independence nor the personal strength to withstand it. For those who did, there was always the Klan, the threat of the mob. The White Citizens Councils may have publicly disclaimed violence, yet they created a climate which made it an ever-present reality.

The Supreme Court itself contributed materially to the success of those who opposed change. The so-called *Brown II* ruling of mid-1955, which supporters of the 1954 decision hoped would lay down a definite timetable mandating its implementation, came as a bitter disappointment to them. While requiring "a prompt and reasonable start toward full compliance," and ruling that desegregation should proceed with "all deliberate speed," the Court gave no further explanation of "full compliance" or "deliberate speed." Some argue that in so doing the Court showed considerable wisdom. Nevertheless in this atmosphere of imprecision, the prospect of delay was wide open to local school boards, and they seized it. NAACP lawyers learned that far from being over, the fight had just begun.

In 1956 the South's political leadership affirmed that there would be no compromise with change. The product of North Carolina Senator Sam Ervin's able legal mind, the "Declaration of Constitutional Principles," or "Southern Manifesto" as it came to be called, was eventually signed by most of the region's senators and representatives. The manifesto condemned the *Brown* decision as unconstitutional, aimed at destroying "amicable relations" between the races. The signatories pledged to have it reversed by "all lawful means" and to ensure that the federal government would never implement desegregation by force. Hailed as marking the beginning of a policy of "massive resistance" in the South, of open defiance of the Supreme Court, the manifesto was in reality a recognition of a course long since set. It symbolized the South's inability to free itself from its history.

Autherine Juanita Lucy was born and grew up in rural Marengo County of southwest Alabama, the last of Minnie and Milton Lucy's ten children. A keen student, she was graduated from Linden Academy, in Linden, Alabama, and then from Miles Memorial College, an all-black school in Birmingham. Unable to secure a teaching position upon graduation, and with the active support of local and state NAACP leaders, she and her friend Pollie Myers decided to improve their qualifications by enrolling at the state's premier public institution, the all-white University of Alabama at Tuscaloosa. Lucy's application for admission to its library science program was received on September 19, 1952, but it was not until February 1956, after three years of complicated legal thrust and counterthrust involving national NAACP intervention, that the university, with great reluctance, finally agreed to her admission. Pollie Myers, by this time, was no longer in the picture, but Autherine Lucy was not alone when she arrived on campus on the miserably cold morning of February 1, 1956. Rather, she was accompanied by a phalanx of NAACP officers and other civil rights activists, including the Reverend Fred Shuttlesworth, later to become a close associate of Martin Luther King, Jr.

Lucy completed the registration process without incident, but that was about the last time her activities on the Tuscaloosa campus could be so characterized. When she attended her first classes on February 3, the student body was tense and the police presence obvious. The previous night Tuscaloosa residents had burned a cross in the front yard of the dean of admissions. That evening, groups of students, chanting, "Hey, hey, ho, ho, Autherine's gotta go," and singing "Dixie," marched downtown. Before being dispersed by local police, they promised more of the same in the days ahead.

The following evening was much more violent. Students and townspeople swarmed over the campus, blatantly defying official pleas for calm. As rebel yells filled the air, demonstrators rocked passing cars and buses, terrorized local blacks, and generally made it clear which way events would move. Photographers got their first chance, as the historian Culpepper Clark has pointed out, "to capture images of a southern mob on the loose"—a depressingly familiar sight in the years ahead. On Monday, February 6, matters got completely out of hand. When Lucy arrived for classes that morning she was greeted by an angry mob, shouting, "Lynch the nigger" and "Keep 'Bama white." Panicky university officials successfully smuggled her off campus, though not before she had been showered with rotten eggs as women shouted "Hit the nigger whore" or simply, "Kill her, kill her." The Klan presence was obvious, no doubt fanning the crowd's viciousness. Lucy, for her part, though badly frightened, remained determined to stick it out. The university had no intention of letting her do so. Asserting its duty to protect students and faculty, the board of trustees decided to "exclude Autherine Lucy until further notice from attending the University of Alabama."

NAACP lawyers moved swiftly in the courts to lift the exclusion order as national attention focused on Tuscaloosa, where the mob had seemingly triumphed. On February 10 the White Citizens Council held its largest-ever rally in Alabama, at which Mississippi's Senator James O. Eastland urged a cheering crowd not "to permit the NAACP to control your state." In such an atmosphere the university's board of trustees decided to bite the bullet and expel Lucy permanently, on the spurious grounds that she had made "scurrilous and scandalous charges" against them of duplicity and double-dealing. This they did on February 29, and despite the best legal efforts of Thurgood Marshall, she was not reinstated. In this, the first real test of the nation's determination to enforce the *Brown* decision, the white South had clearly won. Disorder had prevailed, the Supreme Court had seemingly been defied, and President Eisenhower had looked the other way. During the crisis he made no statement whatsoever about support for federal law. Nor did he do so later the same year when Texas Governor Price Daniel used the Texas Rangers to prevent the court-ordered integration of a high school in Mansfield, Texas. Surely, said the president, the federal government should not be required to intervene in such an obviously local matter. In this context, federal enforcement of the *Brown* decision, and of subsequent court-ordered desegregation, seemed highly unlikely.

Certainly Arkansas Governor Orval Faubus thought so as he embarked on what became the most important challenge to *Brown v. Board of Education*. The location was Little Rock, the trigger, the admission of nine black students to the previously all-white Central High School in the fall of 1957. Arkansas was regarded as a racially moderate state, and Little Rock school superintendent, Virgil Blossom, anticipated no trouble as he began to implement his plan to integrate the city's schools gradually, one grade at a time, with nine carefully selected juniors and seniors as the vanguard. He worked closely with leaders of both the black and white communities to secure acceptance of his ideas. And he believed he had the support of Governor Faubus, supposedly a racial moderate, who had barely mentioned the issue in his successful reelection campaign the previous year. Indeed, those few journalists who bothered to take notice of the preparations in Little Rock all thought they would be using their material to write stories praising the state for not going Alabama's way.

Daisy Bates, head of the local NAACP, was one of the few community leaders to voice apprehension as the opening of the school year neared. Deeply distrustful of Faubus, whom she regarded as weak and pliable, she noted with concern that Central High School's student body comprised the sons and daughters of Little Rock's white working class, not its affluent and presumably more liberal middle- and upper-class communities. The potential of class tensions exacerbating racial feeling was thus a complicating and potentially explosive factor.

Daisy Bates was right about Faubus. As the first day of school approached, he began to shift his ground, showing much less inclination to discuss matters with Blossom or even to talk with the moderates. He was worried about what compliance might do for his political future, and he was subjected to ceaseless pressure to toe the racial line by out-of-state segregationist leaders like Senator Eastland. Moreover, segregationist opinion within Arkansas was hardening fast, and Faubus decided to join the trend. Accordingly he made plans to call out the Arkansas National Guard on September 3, the day school was to begin, ostensibly to prevent violence in the streets but in reality to block the integration mandated by federal court orders.

Given his changed political priorities, Faubus could have written the script for what occurred that day. The Guard ringed the school, the mob swelled and grew more violent, and the children's lives seemed at such risk that their guardians quickly took them home in a group—all except Elizabeth Eckford. She had come to school alone, separated from the rest, and alone she bore the brunt of the mob's anger. "Lynch her," they howled, and lynched she might have been were it not for the bravery of a middle-aged white woman who protected her, standing alone against the crowd until she could get her to a bus. It was a searing first day at school for the fifteen-year-old girl.

What would happen now? Again the federal courts had been defied. Would the president act, or would the mob's action again prove decisive? At first, momentum clearly went with the crowd. The black students did not attend Central High, and Governor Faubus became a national figure, his words and actions reported on national television. He even met with President Eisenhower, who tried to convince him to change his mind but still threatened no federal retaliation if he did not. Clearly the Arkansas governor reveled in the role that Eisenhower's determination to avoid federal intervention had allowed him to play—leader of a defiant South, flaunting the law of the land.

The law, however, eventually caught up with Faubus, and belatedly the president was forced to act. Federal judge Ronald Davies told the governor he would be in contempt if he continued to prevent integration. Faubus then removed the National Guard on September 20, replacing them with city police and thus breaking a promise he had made to the president. The police, predictably, were powerless to contain the passions of the mob, passions which the governor had encouraged since the beginning of the crisis. Local racists had now been joined by segregationists from all over the South, and they were not about to let the crisis fade away.

The nine students reappeared on September 23, by which time the crowd was out of control. By midday they had savagely beaten two black reporters, vandalized the school and its environs, and almost captured the nine students, calling for the lynching of at least one of them. The beleaguered police chief, unable to guarantee their safety while at school, was forced to send the children home. Central High was again segregated, to the cheers of students and their supporters.

For two days the mob took over Little Rock, fulfilling Faubus's prophecy that violence would follow integration. This, rather than any sense of responsibility to federal law, caused the president finally to act—decisively. Rather than use federal marshals to restore order, he decided on riot-trained troops from the 101st Airborne Division, the "Screaming Eagles." "If we have to do this," the president told his attorney general, "then let's apply the best military principles to it and see that the force we send there is strong enough that it will not be challenged." More than a thousand troops were deployed by nightfall, the first soldiers sent to the South since Reconstruction. The integration of Central High took place the next morning under their watchful eye. Faubus had miscalculated badly. Nevertheless it was the governor's misleading of the president, rather than Eisenhower's commitment to the banner of racial justice, that had caused him finally to intervene.

Thus began a most unusual 1957–1958 school year for the students of Central High. The military remained on campus the whole time, those of the nine students who wanted one were assigned their own personal guard to accompany them to and from classes, and to be with them during other times of the day. The military presence, while not reducing the tension of the situation, at least prevented it from escalating into general violence. Nevertheless students and school administrators alike had to deal with a constant flow of abuse, "dirty tricks," and personal acts of confrontation. Every day the students experienced petty harassment, "accidental" pushings, spillages of food in the cafeteria, dousings of ink in class. Yet eight of the nine survived until commencement. One, Minnijean Brown, could not cope. She fought back, she kicked students who kicked her, she threw chili on those who abused her, she talked back—and her grades deteriorated. Eventually she was suspended, the segregationists' only victory for the year. Triumphantly they circulated cards reading "One down. Eight to go."

Governor Faubus had failed to prevent the integration of Central High. He had brought his state into national and international disrepute, and he had rendered himself politically unbeatable. The next year he closed all the city's schools—until the business community threatened to withdraw their political support. Chastened, Faubus quietly reopened them. The Little Rock crisis had shown the world the ugliest aspect of American racism. It offered a chilling example of how quickly demagoguery could promote violence in the absence of strong countervailing power. Nevertheless it also provided a model, however belatedly, for federal action, one which Eisenhower's successor, John F. Kennedy, would be forced to use, equally reluctantly.

A similar outbreak of violence occurred in November 1960 when integration came to New Orleans—"all the more remarkable," as David Goldfield has pointed out, because the school board at least had the Arkansas experience to guide it. As with Little Rock, New Orleans officials decided to begin integration with schools in the city's white working-class districts, rather than those in the more affluent suburbs over which it had control. Because there was little positive community leadership to prepare for the change, as with Little Rock local segregationists took over the controls. "Don't wait for your daughter to be raped by these Congolese," shouted Leander Perez, the segregationist politician from nearby Plaquemines Parish, at a rally on November 14, "do something about it now." Again the mob responded, and again children endured a gauntlet of angry, jeering whites as they sought the education the federal courts had guaranteed. In New Orleans, however, there was no need for troops. The city's business leaders eventually rallied behind the school board, and token integration was peacefully achieved.

If Faubus closed the Little Rock schools only briefly, other Southern governors displayed much more resolution. J. Lindsay Almond of Virginia enthusiastically supported the closing of the whole Prince Edward County school system in 1959. It remained shut for five years while white parents operated a private school system. Blacks received no education at all until the Supreme Court ordered all schools reopened in 1964. In Norfolk, too, the schools were closed for most of 1959. *Life* magazine ran pictures of boys aimlessly cruising the streets and cheerleaders practicing for a football season that would never be. Surely this was not what the Supreme Court had meant by "all deliberate speed."

Most of the South's school boards, cities, and states did not resort either to the fomentation of violence or the shutting down of school systems in order to evade the *Brown* decision. Rather they chose minimum possible compliance, using the courts when they could, stretching the law to its limits, agreeing to tokenism when all else failed. Sometimes business leadership asserted itself to moderate the extremist rantings of the region's politicians. Georgia had a school-closing law, for example, which the governor insisted he would enforce. Atlanta's commercial community persuaded him otherwise. A Little Rock–style confrontation would be extremely bad for business, they argued. In particular, it would frighten away the Northern money the state was trying hard to attract. Thus, when on August 30, 1961, nine black children entered four Atlanta high schools for the first time, the silence was deafening. The absence of violence, and the atmosphere of self-congratulation it engendered, was notable for its rarity.

"Peaceful circumvention" of school integration, as the historian William Chafe convincingly demonstrates, reached "its highest form of sophistication" not in the "massive resistance" states of Virginia, Alabama, Arkansas, or Mississippi but rather in that model of Southern progressivism, North Carolina. There the initial tendency to compliance was subverted by Governor Luther Hodges, not in the strident tones of a Leander Perez but under the guise of moderation. School districts should be perfectly free to integrate if they so wished, he proposed, but if they chose not to do so, or if court-ordered desegregation offended the desires of a particular community, tax funds should be made available to provide alternatives, either on an individual or a community basis. Needless to say, Hodges's plan to use tax dollars to help finance private schools, and to avoid desegregation in other ways, greatly appealed to the white voters of North Carolina. There would be no violence in the state, no confrontation, just inaction, until the courts ruled otherwise, usually in response to NAACP-initiated lawsuits. Meanwhile the pace of desegregation remained well behind that of the more confrontationist states of Virginia, Arkansas, or Texas.

Desegregation in Greensboro, North Carolina, provides, as Chafe says, "a classic example of sophisticated American racism" and of the deliberate frustrations of tokenism. Although it had announced immediately after the *Brown* decision that it planned immediate compliance, the Greensboro school board in fact did nothing until 1957, when six blacks were admitted to previously all-white schools. This was tokenism in action, but it meant that the NAACP could no longer sue either the school board or the state for noncompliance. No further integration followed in Greensboro until 1959, when the NAACP looked like it would win a suit against the school board. The board admitted four more black students to the school specifically named in the suit—but then shifted all white children out of it. Segregation was thus maintained, despite the blacks having been admitted to the school they had sued to attend. In such ways was the *Brown* decision evaded in North Carolina, with much less publicity and confrontation than in Tuscaloosa or Little Rock, yet the effect was exactly the same. By 1960 fewer than 1 percent of the South's black schoolchildren attended integrated schools, and most of these were in the border states. In South Carolina, Alabama, and Mississippi not a single public school was integrated, and no aspiring college student had dared follow Autherine Lucy to Tuscaloosa's leafy campus.

Mississippi, meanwhile, remained a unique "closed society." "In the wake of *Brown*," the historian John Dittmer has written, "white Mississippians had developed a siege mentality so pervasive it encompassed virtually every citizen and institution." The White Citizens Council controlled the state. At the local level its members were especially vigilant in investigating rumors of impending school desegregation moves, promising swift action against anyone stepping out of line. In such a situation even the slightest tokenism was impossible. Indeed, for those few brave activists working for change, implementing the *Brown* decision was not particularly high on their list. Much more important was the right to register to vote. Black Mississippians saw their salvation through the ballot box, not the classroom.

James H. Meredith changed all this. His successful attempt to integrate the University of Mississippi—Ole Miss, as it was locally known—became a signal event, not only in the struggle against segregation in Mississippi but as a symbol for blacks everywhere. It again resulted in a dramatic clash between local and federal power, as President Kennedy, like his predecessor, finally used military might to end continued defiance of federal law. Meredith, a native of Kosciusko, Mississippi, an air force veteran, and a man with a deserved reputation as a "loner," decided in 1960 that he wanted to study law at Ole Miss. He approached the state NAACP for legal aid, should the university prove difficult. Although state secretary Medgar Evers agreed to help him, Meredith had acted entirely on his own. His decision was in no way part of an NAACP priority agenda.

Meredith formally applied for admission to the university early in 1962. Predictably he was refused. The NAACP legal team, led by Constance Baker Motley, then took to the courts, successfully outmaneuvering the university's lawyers throughout the summer. On September 13 the university's options seemed to have run out when the Fifth Circuit Court of Appeals demanded Meredith's immediate enrollment. The crisis seemed to be over.

Those who thought so, however, had not counted on Mississippi's governor, Ross Barnett. A former damages lawyer, an outspoken segregationist, and a White Citizens Council member, Barnett had been elected in 1959, and from then on the Council determined state action. Throughout the summer of 1962, as the courts supported Meredith's application, Barnett's calls for resistance became more and more strident. When, on September 13, the Court of Appeals made its determination, Barnett's response was predictable. Invoking the discredited pre–Civil War doctrine of interposition, he appeared on state television, assuring Mississippi's anxious whites that "no school will be integrated in Mississippi while I am your governor," and insisting that any state official not prepared to go to jail for the cause of segregation should immediately resign. "We will not drink from the cup of genocide," he rather bewilderingly concluded.

President Kennedy and his brother Robert, then attorney general, were apprehensive at this rhetoric of defiance. They had not been enthusiastic about Meredith's decision to attend

Ole Miss, but now they had no option but to support the court decision. Accordingly they engaged in two weeks of secret discussions with Barnett on the terms of Meredith's admission to the university. The governor assured them there would be no trouble, and in their determination, like Eisenhower, to avoid federal intervention, they believed him. As with Faubus before him, Barnett had no intention of keeping his word.

On Tuesday, September 25, U.S. marshals James McShane and John Doar picked up Meredith in New Orleans to escort him to Jackson, the Mississippi capital, where university registrar Robert Ellis had agreed to admit Meredith formally to Ole Miss. They flew into a state marked by collective hysteria. Radio stations aired "Dixie" relentlessly as Barnett continued to preach defiance. When the Meredith party arrived for the formal registration, they found not Ellis but the governor himself, appointed registrar for the day. He solemnly read Meredith his proclamation of interposition, which concluded by finally denying him "admission to the University of Mississippi." Frustrated, Meredith and the marshals retreated to the accompaniment of much abuse, much singing of "Dixie," and the odd rebel yell. So much for the governor's promise to the president. Federal authority had again been defied.

Meredith and the marshals tried again the next morning, this time at the university's main campus at Oxford. Again they were denied access to the university, their way blocked by ranks of state troopers and sheriffs. By this time commentators were comparing the confrontation to those at Little Rock, or even Fort Sumter, and the White House could not afford to let it go on much longer. Robert Kennedy continued to negotiate with Barnett, hoping to arrange a scenario whereby the governor appeared to yield reluctantly to superior force, without a wholesale mobilization of federal troops. Meanwhile the mob gathered in Oxford, the Confederate flag was everywhere in evidence, and FBI reports indicated that racists were converging from far and wide. In New Orleans, on Friday, September 28, a Fifth Circuit panel found Governor Barnett guilty, in absentia, of contempt, sentencing him to prison unless Meredith was immediately registered.

On the next day, Saturday, September 29, President Kennedy himself talked at length with Barnett, trying to arrange a deal. Nothing worked. That evening the governor spoke at the halftime break of the Ole Miss–Kentucky football game. "I love Mississippi," he roared into the microphones. "I love her people. I love our customs." The crowd's frenzy at these three short sentences persuaded the Kennedys that further negotiations were useless, that Barnett simply could not be trusted to keep his word. The president at long last prepared to use the army if he had to, and decided to address the nation on the crisis the following evening.

Sunday in Oxford was crisp and clear, but the mood of the mob which had gathered on the Ole Miss campus was decidedly ugly. All day tensions grew, the more so as reports filtered through of troops and military equipment flying into the town's airport. At 6 p.m. Meredith arrived from Memphis and was smuggled into a deserted residence hall for the night, before another registration attempt the next day. He was protected not by troops but—still attempting to avoid confrontation—by a band of federal marshals with orders to kill anyone directly threatening Meredith but otherwise to be as unobtrusive as possible. Meanwhile Kennedy prepared for his national address, in which he intended to discuss the importance of the rule of law and how, despite everything, it had prevailed in this crisis and violence had been avoided.

The speech was one of Kennedy's finest, but he made his appeal for conciliation unaware that the Oxford campus had already become a battleground. Even before the president spoke, the angry crowd, inflamed by the rhetoric of super-patriots like General Edwin Walker, had begun to attack the lightly armed marshals with bricks, bottles, and Molotov cocktails. Once the president announced that Meredith was already on campus, this fury was uncontrolled, and some in the crowd started shooting. Again Barnett broke his word, removing all state troopers from the campus, thus effectively throwing the marshals to the mob. Outnumbered, denied permission to fire back, they could only await the arrival of troops. Not until 2:15 a.m. the following morning did the first soldiers appear. By this time 2 men lay dead and 160 marshals had been injured; 28 bore gunshot wounds. The campus was a war zone, and Oxford, Mississippi, was the new international symbol of American racism. It was an American tragedy, and like Little Rock before it, one that could have been avoided had the White House acted with more resolve from the start, instead of trying to make deals with Southern racist politicians.

Quickly the army restored order. By morning, calm of a sort had returned to Oxford. Meredith was duly registered as a student, escorted to the administration building by a military guard, and attended his first class that same morning, in American history. The soldiers stayed with him throughout the year, but Ole Miss soon disappeared from the front pages and television screens because of the gathering Cuban missile crisis. If *Brown v. Board of Education* had finally come to Mississippi, it had done so at terrible cost, not the least of which was to the image of the White House. Moreover, Meredith's presence on campus did not markedly alter the tolerance level of Mississippi's young. He was alternately abused and shamed during his year there; those few students who treated him decently were themselves harassed. The high hopes of 1954 had never seemed more unrealistic than in James Meredith's wake.

George Corley Wallace, the "fighting judge" from Barbour County, Alabama, had not entered Alabama politics as a rabid segregationist. Rather, this political protégé of "Kissing Jim" Folsom had built a reputation as a friend of organized labor, with relatively progressive views. Defeat in the Democratic gubernatorial primary of 1958, when John Patterson garnered both the White Citizens Council vote and an electoral victory, changed all that. Wallace spent the next four years shedding his progressive mantle, reinventing himself as the apotheosis of segregation. Opening his primary campaign in March 1962, he pledged himself to oppose all attempts to integrate Alabama's schools. "And when the court order comes," he shouted, he would refuse to abide by it, "even to the point of standing in the schoolhouse door, if necessary." Any black students who wanted to take what the law said was theirs would have to push by him. The crowd loved this promise, as they did all of Wallace's uncompromisingly segregationist views, and he easily defeated his erstwhile mentor, the bumbling, drunken, but still essentially decent Folsom.

Wallace had to make good on his promise a year later. As in 1956, the contested area was the University of Alabama. What had happened in neighboring Oxford had concentrated the minds of both university officials and state politicians. In the changing racial climate, it was only a matter of time before someone attempted to follow Autherine Lucy. In such a situation, would Wallace provoke a federal-state confrontation similar to that brought on by Ross Barnett, with the same inevitable outcome?

Vivian Juanita Malone had been born in 1942 to a family that prized education above most else. Her brothers had attended Tuskegee Institute, but Vivian had her heart set on the University of Alabama, where she hoped to study accounting.

She had applied in 1960 to its Mobile Center but had been rejected. Now, in 1962, and with NAACP advice, she decided to try again, this time at the university's main Tuscaloosa campus.

James A. Hood, an outstanding high school athlete and scholar from Gadsden, Alabama, had aspirations of becoming a clinical psychologist. An A student at Atlanta's Clark College in 1962, he had become dissatisfied with the program there, and he too decided that Tuscaloosa was where he wanted to be. Again, with NAACP help, he made the application which, with Malone's, would give the governor the chance to make good his campaign promise.

Wallace lost no time in making it clear to the university's board of trustees that he was in earnest. He would redeem his campaign pledge, he asserted; he would "stand in the schoolhouse door." Nevertheless he had no interest in provoking the sort of mob action that had occurred in Oxford, and in the end he knew the courts would prevail. What he was talking about was a gesture of defiance, a gesture he would make alone. Thus instructed, and most relieved to be off the hook, university officials prepared for integration.

By May, Wallace had changed his mind. There was to be no integration without a court order, he declared, effectively blocking the trustees' plans to avoid litigation and bow to the inevitable. Various legal maneuvering followed, with the governor and the university often at cross-purposes. Meanwhile the White House made it quite clear that in the event of another confrontation there would be no holding back on troops this time. By early June, when the summer term was due to begin, the federal courts had made the issue crystal clear. Malone and Hood were to be registered as students of the university on June 11, and the governor was enjoined against further interference. Klansmen gathered in Tuscaloosa during the weekend, but they were quickly neutralized by 750 state troopers sent to prevent violence. The Kennedys, for their part, made plans to federalize the Alabama National Guard as the tableau was played out.

On Monday, June 10, Nicholas Katzenbach, deputy attorney general, arrived in Tuscaloosa to make sure the script would be followed as written. When Malone and Hood arrived at the university the next day, he was with them. There they found George Wallace, true to his word, blocking entrance to the registration building. Katzenbach asked him for his "unequivocal assurance" that he would let the university enroll the students. The governor denounced the federal government's "unwelcomed, unwanted, unwarranted, and force-induced intrusion upon the campus of the University of Alabama," and refused to stand aside. Katzenbach and the students then withdrew, the two young people to rest in a dorm, the federal officer to tell the president it was time to federalize the National Guard.

General Henry V. Graham, the Guard's commander, was swiftly apprised of Kennedy's decision. That afternoon, when Katzenbach, Malone, and Hood returned to the campus, he was with them, along with troop carriers, motorcycle police, and enough infantrymen to make crowd violence unlikely. At 3:30 p.m. the drama reached its climax. Wallace again positioned himself in the doorway, whereupon General Graham asked him to step aside, "on order of the President of the United States." The governor made a statement bitterly denouncing the federalization of the Guard, called for calm, and then did as Graham had asked. Hood and Malone entered "the schoolhouse door" to scattered cheers. Within fifteen minutes they were registered as students of the university, and the crisis was over. Learning from the Oxford disaster, the federal government had displayed much more resolve in enforcing *Brown* while Wallace had recognized the inevitable; yet once more the face of Southern intransigence was there for all to see. Fortunately there had been no violence.

Governor Wallace did not turn up at the university's Huntsville campus two days later when a third African American, David McGlathery, presented himself, along with Katzenbach, for enrollment. He was accommodated without a hitch. Nor did Wallace stand defiant in Birmingham in September, where the city was under a federal court order to admit five black students to three public schools. He did, however, send the National Guard to block their entry. Again President Kennedy moved decisively. He federalized the Guard, then withdrew it, allowing the black students to attend their first classes. Public school integration had thus begun in Alabama. Governor Wallace by now had his mind set on other things. Having established himself as the South's most strident opponent of federal enforcement of desegregation, he decided to try for higher office. On September 13, 1963, he announced his candidacy for the presidency in 1964.

Black and white children went to school together for the first time in the fall of 1963 in cities other than Birmingham, Alabama. Boards of education throughout the region were running out of legal maneuvers to stay the inevitable; the federal courts were seeing to that, albeit terribly slowly. By the end of the year Mississippi alone still maintained entirely separate public school systems, and even her days were numbered as suits filed by black parents slowly moved through the courts. Throughout the region, black activism was on the increase, and the quickened pace of desegregation suits was one result. Moreover, Little Rock, New Orleans, and Ole Miss had brought home to Southern business communities the cost of riots and disorder. Tuscaloosa businessmen in 1963, for example, while understanding the need for Governor Wallace to play out his charade, were at pains to ensure that there would not be a repeat of the previous year's violence at Oxford, Mississippi. Slowly and painfully, the *Brown* decision was at last being implemented.

Nevertheless it also had to be said that, in the fall of 1963, nearly ten years after the Supreme Court had outlawed public school desegregation, only 1.17 percent of black schoolchildren in the eleven states of the old Confederacy were attending school with whites. At that rate, it would take 1,288 years for the South to integrate all its schools—a timetable, as David Goldfield drily remarked, "that imparted novel meaning to the phrase 'all deliberate speed.'" The schoolhouse door may have been breached a crack, but it had certainly not been flung open wide. New and decisive action was required from courts, communities, and legislatures before that would occur.

3

"I Have a Dream"

WHEN SHE BOARDED her regular bus on Thursday, December 1, 1955, after leaving work for the day—she was a seamstress in Montgomery, Alabama's leading department store—Rosa Parks had nothing more serious in mind than getting home to her family as quickly as possible. All thirty-six seats were soon filled—blacks seated from the rear, as local segregation ordinances stipulated, whites from the front. The driver noticed that a white man was standing, and he called for the four black passengers in the row just behind the whites to move to the back of the bus, again according to local ordinances. No one responded, whereupon the driver, J. P. Blake, stopped the bus. "You better make it light on yourselves and let me have those seats," he told the recalcitrant four. Three of them immediately got up. Mrs. Parks did not. She had not sat down in the white section, she claimed, and therefore had no need to lose her seat. Blake threatened her with arrest, but to no avail. He left the bus, returning with two police officers who quickly took her to jail. She had just made her imprint on American history.

What had happened to Mrs. Parks that day could in no way have been planned, yet she was no ordinary Montgomery citizen. A deeply religious, highly respected member of the town's black community, she had also been active for years in the local NAACP chapter and was currently serving as its secretary. She had been introduced to the NAACP by the town's most prominent black activist, E. D. Nixon. A giant of a man physically, and with the courage to match his stature, Nixon was president both of the Alabama branch of the Brotherhood of Sleeping Car Porters and of the local chapter of the NAACP. Everyone in Montgomery, black and white alike, knew Nixon, and in their various ways most respected him. He was also close to the town's few white liberals, most notably the old New Dealers Aubrey Williams and Clifford Durr, now a Montgomery attorney. Nixon had introduced Mrs. Parks to these two pariahs. She did some sewing for Durr's outspoken wife Virginia, once a member of the SCHW's anti–poll tax committee, while Williams had arranged her attendance at a recent school for citizenship at the Highlander Folk School. Prophetically, the day before her arrest Mrs. Parks had sent a letter of appointment to the most recent member of the NAACP chapter's executive committee. This was a young minister just arrived in town to take over the Dexter Avenue Baptist Church. His name was Martin Luther King, Jr.

News of Mrs. Parks's arrest quickly reached E. D. Nixon. Deeply concerned, he telephoned Clifford Durr, and the pair decided to go to the jail immediately to make bond. Mrs. Durr insisted on going along as well. Bond was easily arranged, and soon Mrs. Parks was safe at home with her husband and her desperately worried mother. Only then did Nixon voice what had been on his mind the past hour. The NAACP had been planning for months to test the city's segregation statutes, specifically challenging the bus ordinances. On two previous occasions they thought they had found their incident, only to find problems with the particular defendants. Mrs. Parks was different: highly respected by the black community, yet humble enough to make a good impression on the white judges into whose hands she would be committed. Nixon asked her there and then if she would do it. Her husband Raymond was bitterly opposed, as was her mother. "The white folks will kill you, Rosa," a terrified Raymond Parks asserted. Rosa Parks, however, was made of stern stuff indeed. "If you think it will mean something to Montgomery and do some good, I'll be happy to go along with it," she told Nixon. Thus began the Montgomery Bus Boycott, one of the defining events of the civil rights revolution.

Upon returning home, Nixon got on the telephone to spread the word. One of the many he spoke to was Fred Gray, a young black attorney, who quickly agreed to represent Parks. Gray had several friends in Montgomery's most active black political group outside the NAACP, the Women's Political Council. He phoned them immediately, including its leader Jo Ann Robinson, an English professor at Alabama State University and a canny organizer and operator. The WPC was also active in the affairs of the Dexter Avenue Church, which was how its new young preacher first became involved in the protest. Robinson met with her colleagues at midnight to draft a letter of protest at Mrs. Parks's arrest. As they talked, one idea took hold. Her case would be called the following Monday. Why not, therefore, ask every black citizen to stay off the buses that day in solidarity and protest? Could they spread the word in time? It was, after all, already early Friday morning. They decided to work the rest of the night to produce a leaflet which could then be distributed in black churches that Sunday.

Around 3 a.m. Robinson alerted E. D. Nixon as to their plan. Nixon agreed with the idea of the Monday bus boycott and telephoned a few local ministers to put them in the picture. One call went to Martin Luther King; Nixon needed his centrally located church as the venue for a planning meeting later that Friday. After some thought, King agreed. Indeed, he helped contact some of the fifty community leaders who eventually met in the basement of his church, agreed to go ahead with a one-day boycott that Monday, and drafted a new leaflet explaining the reasons for the stand. Significantly the leaders also decided to hold a mass meeting on Monday evening to decide on future action.

Thousands of leaflets circulated through the black community that weekend. Joe Azbell, city editor of the *Montgomery Advertiser*, helped spread the word by running a story detailing the planned boycott. That Monday Montgomery's buses were empty. Thousands of blacks who responded to the call walked, hitched rides, or car-pooled to their destinations. Rosa Parks was duly convicted later in the morning. Fred Gray filed a notice of appeal, and Nixon left the courthouse in order to post bond. A crowd of more than five hundred awaited him, ready to storm the courthouse itself should Mrs. Parks be threatened in any way. That was the moment, Nixon later reminisced, that he realized there would be no turning back. Montgomery's black citizens had had enough of segregation.

That afternoon the black leadership group met to plan the evening's mass meeting. Already there was gathering support for a continuation of the boycott, given its unexpectedly high level of support. A permanent organization was therefore necessary. The name came easily—the Montgomery Improvement Association. There was some jockeying for the position of president, but in the end there was only one nomination, that of Martin Luther King. More senior community leaders, including Nixon and the Reverend Ralph Abernathy decided to stand aside for the young man, convinced that his very newness to the city, his lack of roots there, of established friendships or enmities, would be assets in holding the community together. Besides, if things went wrong, he would find it easier to leave. And so he was chosen to lead, a choice ratified by the mass meeting that evening. There he gave his first political speech. When King told the gathering, "You know, my friends, there comes a time when people get tired of being trampled over by the iron feet of oppression," the cheers and applause were thunderous. When he spoke of raising "the weapon of protest," protest without violence, protest in the name of Christian love; when, in concluding, he spoke of the community's determination "to work and fight until justice runs down like water, and righteousness like a mighty stream," he not only defined the rhetorical cadences of the civil rights struggle but the context within which it would be waged. As the historian Taylor Branch commented, that first speech made King "forever a public person." He was twenty-six years old.

Martin Luther King's background and upbringing were hardly that of a typical Southern black man. For one thing, he was a child of the upper middle class. Born in Atlanta, where his family was among the most prominent and respected of the city's black population, his early life was as insulated from the ravages of segregation as it was possible to be. He was born, too, into the bosom of the church. His maternal grandfather, the Reverend A. D. Williams, had both established the Ebenezer Baptist Church and turned it into Atlanta's leading black congregation, a congregation which his father, the Reverend Martin Luther ("Daddy") King, Sr., took over in due course.

Young Martin was educated as befitted a son of privilege and influence, first at Atlanta's prestigious Morehouse College, and then, contrary to his father's wishes, at Pennsylvania's Crozer Theological Seminary, one of the nation's most liberal institutions, and in Boston University's Ph.D. program. In recent years consideration of King's higher education has been bedeviled by well-documented charges that some of his written assignments at both Crozer and Boston, including his dissertation, were plagiarized. Be that as it may, it is clear that these years of study broadened him considerably, moving him away from the fundamentalist, intensely personal theology of his father. As a student he became deeply influenced by the work of Walter Rauschenbusch, the mission of the social gospel, and the possibilities of a theological basis for the pursuit of social justice. In these years, too, King first became attracted to the ideas of Mohandas Gandhi, and especially to the Indian leader's notions of nonviolent resistance to injustice. Gandhi, he later wrote, in an oft-quoted sentence, was the first figure in history "to lift the love ethic of Jesus above mere interaction between individuals to a powerful and effective social force on a grand scale." Although Gandhi and Rauschenbusch remained the two most powerful influences on King's thought, Reinhold Niebuhr's pessimism also taught him an important truth. Himself a social reformer, Niebuhr nevertheless was under no delusions as to the pervasive presence of evil in the world. Thus while regarding the social gospel ideal as worth pursuing, he had little expectation that the Kingdom of God would ever be established on earth. Through Niebuhr, King learned to temper his optimism. He always knew full well the power of the evil forces he had joined in battle.

When King decided to return to the South, it was not to Atlanta and to Ebenezer, as his father had confidently assumed. Rather, in 1954 he accepted the call to Dexter Avenue in Montgomery. From there he began his journey to national greatness. He brought with him to Montgomery his new bride, Coretta Scott, a young woman of exceptional musical ability and ambition who by hard work and talent had moved from her rural Alabama roots to graduate study at the New England Conservatory of Music. Now her new husband was bringing her back to the South, a move she could only regard with the greatest apprehension. Her life, too, would soon be altered permanently.

From the beginning the Montgomery Improvement Association offered to negotiate with the bus company to end the boycott. Its initial demands were modest indeed: *one*, that the bus drivers display common courtesy to their black patrons; *two*, that passengers be seated on a first-come, first-served basis, blacks sitting from the rear of the bus to the front, whites from the front to the back; and *three*, that the company begin to employ black drivers on mainly black routes. Such demands were scarcely revolutionary. Similar arrangements were already operating in a number of Southern cities, and certainly they did not represent a serious challenge to segregation. The bitter, unyielding opposition of the bus company, of the city administration, and of Montgomery's white citizens is thus difficult to comprehend—except that the fight was about symbols, not actualities. As Jack Crenshaw, the bus company's attorney, asserted in a heated discussion with King, "If we granted the Negroes these demands, they would go about boasting of a victory they had won over the white people; and this we will not stand for." This was the nub of the matter, as King quickly came to realize. As he wrote, these early discussions taught him two valuable lessons, both of which drew him back to Niebuhr. The first was that people do not surrender privileges easily, no matter how reasonable the demands made of them. The second went to the very heart of segregation itself. Its real purpose, King learned, was never simply to separate the races but rather to oppress the segregated blacks. Thus an end to oppression, true equality, could come only with an end to segregation itself.

The boycott was not settled early. Instead the bus company drastically reduced services to black neighborhoods. This not only hardened the black community's resolve, it also meant that those blacks who wavered, especially when the winter rains came, found there were no buses to ride.

Meanwhile King and the MIA kept up the community's spirit, mainly through frequent mass rallies. As the boycott gained national attention, money began to arrive from around the country, from individual blacks and black organizations, from white liberal communities, and even from outside the United States. The resources to provide alternative means of transportation were soon there, including a fleet of station wagons paid for by the MIA, which also arranged car pools and multiple taxi hires. Nevertheless most blacks continued to walk, more through preference than necessity. It was their visible protest against the oppression that had shaped their lives. The frequently quoted responses of two women when refusing proffered rides graphically makes this point. "I'm not walking for myself," said one, "but for my children and grandchildren." Said an elderly walker, obviously footsore and weary, "My feet is tired, but my soul is at rest." Nothing better captured the dignity and resolution of Montgomery's black citizens than that remark.

As the weeks lengthened into months, Martin Luther King, as leader of the MIA, found himself a hated symbol for Montgomery's whites. He was abused and frequently threatened, his house was bombed, and on two occasions he was arrested on trumped-up charges. Through it all he displayed the courage and faith, the disregard of self, that was to characterize his later leadership. He also displayed his capacity for hard work and for charting broad plans and strategies, and, above all, his ability to move people, to inspire them through the power of the spoken word. No other American political figure in the twentieth century, with the exception of Franklin Roosevelt, used the public podium as effectively as King.

Thus the boycott continued into 1956 with the MIA reaffirming its willingness to negotiate, and the white community determined to avoid concession. The town's mayor, W. A. "Tacky" Gayle, at one point attempted to bypass King and the MIA and negotiate with other, more pliant members of the black community. But this tactic quickly backfired. Most of Montgomery's city officials, including Gayle and Police Commissioner Clyde Sellers, had by this time joined the White Citizens Council, which urged a campaign of economic intimidation against blacks and any whites thought sympathetic to the boycott. Gayle was particularly angered by women like Virginia Durr, who persisted in driving their maids to and fro each day. "The Negroes have made their own bed," he said, "and the whites should let them sleep in it."

By February 1956 both sides had taken the dispute to the courts. As well as Rosa Parks's appeal, Fred Gray had filed a federal suit asking that local and state regulations requiring segregation be declared unconstitutional. At the same time a county grand jury began to consider the city's contention that the boycott was an illegal conspiracy against the bus company. Of course the law could not compel anyone to patronize a business, Judge Eugene Carter told the jurors. Nevertheless the right to conduct a business free of illegal interference was "a valuable property right" deserving of protection. If the grand jury found the boycott illegal, they should indict its leaders. The jury did exactly that. On February 21 it identified and indicted 115 black citizens—"the dumbest act," Montgomery journalist Grover Hall later asserted, "ever done in Montgomery." In so doing the grand jury made quite clear its position on segregation. In Alabama, its message stated, "we are committed to segregation by custom and by law; we intend to maintain it. The settlement of differences over school attendance, public transportation and other public facilities must be made within these laws which reflect our way of life."

Whites were jubilant at the indictments, believing that the conviction of those named would end the boycott. Blacks, certain that their own suit would be successful, were not at all fazed by the arrest of their leaders. King was the first of them to be tried, a month later. Judge Carter heard the case without a jury. The prosecution had little difficulty proving a boycott existed and that King was involved in it. But the charge that the conspirators had broken the law through their advocacy of violence was undercut by the testimony of whites such as Joe Azbell, who contended that King had consistently urged the opposite. He was convicted nevertheless and offered the choice of a $500 fine or 386 days at hard labor. He posted bond and appealed.

The arrests and King's trial kept the boycott where the MIA wanted it, at the forefront of national attention. The news media highlighted the testimony of the defense witnesses that they had been cursed, spat upon, beaten, and even shot at by white bus drivers. On the lawn outside the courthouse, as news of King's conviction reached them, blacks sang, "We ain't gonna ride the buses no more." Nor did they.

On June 4 a three-judge federal district court handed down its ruling on Gray's suit. Finding that segregation on a common carrier violated the Fourteenth Amendment, it enjoined Gayle from enforcing bus segregation but stayed the effect of the decision until Montgomery officials had appealed the case to the Supreme Court. The city, now desperate, fought the boycott with heightened ferocity. The state outlawed the NAACP, claiming it was a foreign corporation which had ignored Alabama's registration laws. At the same time the city obtained an indictment against the MIA for operating a business—the car pool—without a license. White supremacists throughout the region continued to press city officials not to give an inch.

King was worried by the indictment and the prospect that the city's application for an injunction to stop the car pool would be successful. He knew that without the car pool, both as a symbol and an alternative means of transportation, the boycott would be much more difficult to sustain. Thus he awaited the court deliberations scheduled for November 13 with considerable apprehension. Just before Judge Carter opened them, however, a reporter handed him a note that rendered the proceeding irrelevant. It read thus: "The United States Supreme Court today affirmed a decision of a special three-judge U.S. district court in declaring Alabama's state and local laws requiring segregation on buses unconstitutional." It was "a joyous daybreak," shouted the jubilant King. "God Almighty has spoken from Washington, D.C.," someone else cried. Judge Carter, as expected, granted the city its injunction. It no longer mattered.

The next evening ten thousand blacks met to end the boycott officially. When the vote was taken, there was a mighty shout. "All over the floor," as Lerone Bennett reported, "men and women were on their feet, waving handkerchiefs and weeping." Theirs was a mighty victory, the first for Southern blacks since the Civil War. Its architect, the diffident young preacher, would henceforth stride the national stage. All over the region, fired by his example, other black communities would find similar courage. That was the enduring meaning of the boycott: the example it provided for the future.

That same night the Klan appeared in Montgomery's black neighborhoods. Fully hooded and gowned, a procession of the sort that normally struck terror into black hearts wound slowly through the streets. That night, however, there was no fear. Instead some blacks actually followed the Klansmen, laughing, applauding ironically, and hurling insults. For once it was the Klan's turn to slink away, thoroughly discomfited, into the night. As King later commented, "a once fear-ridden people had been transformed" by the boycott, and there would be no changing back.

Montgomery's blacks had to keep walking for one more month, for that was how long it took for the official word of the Supreme Court decision to reach city officials. Finally, at 6 a.m. on December 21, 1956, King and his companions boarded a local bus and sat in the front seats, an event of international significance. The boycott, begun as an attempt to win better treatment within the confines of segregation ordinances, had ended with the Court sweeping them away.

Martin Luther King, as the historian Harvard Sitkoff has commented, became "a worldwide symbol of African-American determination" as a consequence of the boycott. He received countless speaking engagements, was written about, talked about, and given prizes and awards. He appeared at the 1956 Democratic convention, with both the president and vice-president, and represented his country at Ghana's 1957 independence ceremonies. In 1958 he survived a serious assassination attempt, an unwelcome consequence of fame. Above all, in those first years after Montgomery he both deepened his nonviolent philosophy and developed an organization through which he could work to continue the struggle against segregation.

During the boycott King's rhetoric had appealed to the Christian beliefs of his people. Thus the struggle was to be waged with love and forgiveness in their hearts, turning the other cheek at all times. But his uncompromising opposition to violence had a deeply practical side as well. In the Deep South, where whites held all the power, violence would have been suicidal. In his later speeches and workshops, King began to emphasize Gandhian principles and practices. He used films of Gandhi's movement, produced little plays built around incidents in Gandhi's campaign, and adapted Gandhian songs to a Southern context. Aided by such disciples of the Mahatma as Bayard Rustin and Glenn Smiley, King fused his own Christianity, Gandhian nonviolence, and his (King's) awareness of the potential power of militant mass protest into an ideology of resistance suited to the Southern context, "nonviolent direct action." At its core was a variation of the old adage, "Hate the sin, love the sinner." King's focus was always on the system of segregation; he never attacked individual segregationists. He took account of white feelings of guilt and forced whites to face the evil of segregation, but without fear of violent reprisal. Above all, King stressed that if his movement succeeded, the victory would not belong to him or to blacks alone, but to all Americans.

His message, then, was at once one of reconciliation and of no compromise with the evil of white supremacy. "To accept passively an unjust system," he wrote, "is to cooperate with that system; thereby the oppressed become as evil as the oppressor. Noncooperation with evil is as much a moral obligation as is cooperation with good." Apathy was the prime sin in such a situation, not aggressive, nonviolent protest. Perhaps too much has been made of King's conversion to the principles of *satyagraha*.* He continued to talk chiefly in the cadences of the Scriptures, and the bulk of his examples were always biblical. The Greek concept of *agape*, a general em-

**Satyagraha* was Gandhi's approach to nonviolent resistance, which he believed should involve more than mere passivity. Rather, it could be strong, forceful, even aggressive, with the aim of provoking confrontation in order to make a moral point and raise political awareness. It gave unity to his long campaign against British rule in India.

bracing love of all people everywhere, remained central to his thought. What can be said with certainty is that he provided, in nonviolent direct action, the spiritual and ideological means for Southern blacks to fight for their freedom while at the same time exciting the imagination, and in time the commitment, of thousands of white supporters. It was a superb achievement.

The organization that King formed, and through which he planned to wage the struggle, was the Southern Christian Leadership Conference (SCLC). Radicalized by the Montgomery experience, ministers throughout the South planned antisegregation campaigns of their own. Modeling his tactics on King's, the Reverend Charles K. Steele, for example, led a successful boycott of the Tallahassee, Florida, bus system. Similar boycotts occurred in Atlanta and Savannah. In Tuskegee, Alabama, working closely with King, the Reverend C. G. Gomillion led a campaign against white merchants to prevent black disfranchisement. The Montgomery momentum was obvious. In order to capitalize on it and to coordinate these various activities, in February 1957 nearly one hundred black ministers met in New Orleans to form the Southern Christian Leadership Conference. King was elected its first president, and his loyal lieutenant, Ralph Abernathy, its secretary. Its founding symbolized a shift in the wellspring of black resistance to racism from the North to the South, and from the courts to direct action. The Southern black church, as Sitkoff has observed, "would become preeminent in leading black resistance to white oppression, and they would do so by preaching the virtues of massive nonviolent protest." The SCLC always worked closely with the NAACP, but it had its own agenda.

The SCLC was formed in a climate of optimism, but in its first three years its accomplishments were few, particularly in leading direct-action campaigns. This was in large part due to the intransigence of Southern whites: in the late 1950s massive resistance was at its strongest, and economic intimidation and raw violence were commonplace. The few civil rights victories achieved in those years came through the courts and the legal tactics of the NAACP, and some even began to question the utility of King's nonviolent message. Robert Williams, head of the Monroe, North Carolina, NAACP branch, was dismissed for arming fifty of his members, forming them into a gun club, and then engaging in a shoot-out with Klansmen. Upon his dismissal, Williams poured scorn on nonviolence, advocating instead that blacks wage defensive guerrilla warfare.

Organizational difficulties and office rivalries also hampered SCLC's efficacy. King, who shuttled between Montgomery and the SCLC office in Atlanta, and around whom the structure was created, was frequently absent from either city. Without him the organization often appeared leaderless, unsure of policy or direction. This was despite the best efforts of its second executive director, the veteran activist Ella Baker. She had gone to Atlanta in 1958, planning to stay only long enough to get the organization off the ground and launch its first activity, a voter registration program, pending the appointment of a permanent executive director. But the man offered the job proved so unsatisfactory that King soon asked for his resignation, and Baker agreed to take over. Initially she worked single-handed. "There was no machinery, no staff, except me," she recalled. She received little encouragement from King, preoccupied as he was with his speaking engagements and his writing, and often encountered active hostility from other ministers on the administrative committee. She particularly resented their condescending attitude toward women, a fault from which not even King was immune. Nevertheless

Baker persisted, and slowly both a structure and a program took shape. In 1959 King agreed to resign his Dexter Avenue position and move to Atlanta, so as to devote more time to SCLC matters. Late that year, acting on the advice of Stanley Levinson (a New York attorney with, it was later revealed, close ties to the Communist party) he appointed the veteran activist Bayard Rustin as director of public relations. There was some risk in doing so, given Rustin's avowed homosexuality and his own connections with the Communist party, and in 1960 Rustin quietly resigned his position rather than face public exposure. He remained extremely influential behind the scenes, however, providing the organizational expertise that King lacked.

Ella Baker also departed in 1960, to be replaced by the ambitious, energetic, and self-promoting Wyatt T. Walker, who forged close links between SCLC and the Highlander Folk School. Highlander transferred its complete citizenship training programs, which included voter education and registration, to King's organization, thus giving it a focus. Before her departure in 1960, however, Baker made a final important contribution to SCLC's future by involving the organization with the new phenomenon of student protest exemplified by the sit-in movement of that year. She was instrumental in organizing a conference of student activists, financed by the SCLC, with King as the keynote speaker. There he urged them to set up a permanent organization to build on the momentum of the sit-ins. As a direct result, the Student Nonviolent Coordinating Committee (SNCC) was created. If King had hoped SNCC would become a branch of SCLC, he was to be disappointed. The students preferred to maintain their independence from the ministers, and they never wholeheartedly accepted nonviolence as a philosophy rather than simply a tactic. Nevertheless the two organizations were able to work together in reasonable harmony for some years, and it was during this time that the walls of segregation were decisively breached.

Because of this connection, in fact, King found himself in jail in October 1960, and thus became an influential figure in the presidential election campaign then nearing a climax. Earlier in the year King had been arrested in Georgia for driving with an out-of-state license and placed on probation. When he was again arrested in October for joining SNCC's Julian Bond and several others in a sit-in at a leading Atlanta department store, he was charged with breaking probation and sentenced to four months' jail. Blacks met this news with consternation, apprehension, and anger. Its significance was not lost on the two presidential candidates, especially after King had been secretly taken from the De Kalb County jail to the grim state penitentiary at Reidsville. Nixon, fearful of losing white Southern votes, decided against any action. John F. Kennedy's response is well known. He telephoned the distraught Mrs. King, assured her of his concern, and asked if he could do anything to help. Meanwhile his campaign manager and brother, Robert, pulled every string he could to secure King's early release, including speaking personally to the sentencing judge. How decisive his influence was is not clear. Certainly King was given another hearing and released on bond, pending an appeal on the original traffic violation. Delighted, "Daddy" King, a lifelong Republican, announced that he had a suitcase full of votes which would be going to the Democrats. Given the closeness of the election result, and the fact that a last-minute switch of black voters away from Nixon provided the victory margin, Kennedy's intervention was clearly decisive.

Martin Luther King went to jail again in Georgia in 1961 and 1962, this time in Albany, in the southwest part of the state. Charles Sherrod, SNCC's first field secretary, just twenty-two years of age, had been encouraged to establish a voter registration project there. In Albany he found an enthusiastic group of young blacks, anxious for a wide-ranging confrontation, and a rather skeptical black community leadership, most of them deeply involved with the NAACP. Sherrod decided to ignore the older group and work exclusively with the town's high school and college students. Their citywide campaign began in November 1961. For more than a year thousands of young blacks marched in Albany, picketed local stores, sat-in at lunch counters, and demonstrated at the local voter registration office in a massive assault on segregation. More than a thousand of them were jailed as a consequence, yet nothing changed. By the end of 1962 Albany was still a completely segregated city, one in which only a few blacks could vote. Why had the campaign failed so badly?

One reason was because its organizers, perhaps naively, had expected the federal government to move decisively whenever federal laws were broken, as they clearly had been throughout the long campaign. The Kennedys, however, were not of a mind to do so, provided local officials could maintain the peace with a minimum of violence. Here the chief of police, Laurie Pritchett, was pivotal. He was no stereotypical Southern racist cop but a highly intelligent man who had studied King's writings, among other things, and who knew how important national media attention was in keeping pressure on localities. Nothing excited the media more than white violence against peaceful demonstrators. Indeed, King's philosophy depended on such images to elicit white sympathy and support. Pritchett therefore determined that there would be no violence in Albany. Demonstrators would be arrested, of course, and jails would be filled, but there would be no mistreatment of prisoners. In particular there would be no mobs, no repeats of Little Rock. Anyone practicing or even advocating violence against the demonstrators would be promptly punished, that Pritchett made quite clear. He always seemed to be one step ahead of the SNCC activities; he always seemed to know their plans. Worried, Sherrod assumed his phone was tapped, but actually the police chief relied mainly on reports from adult members of the black community itself.

Eventually a truce was effected between the young activists and senior members of Albany's black professional community, lead by osteopath William G. Anderson, who began to support the mass action campaign. It did not seem to do much good. Four hundred and seventy-one demonstrators were jailed on December 6, many of them held in neighboring counties, yet the city officials showed no sign of negotiating. In this context Dr. Anderson, realizing that the SNCC people had bitten off much more than they could chew, decided to seek assistance from King and his SCLC. King agreed to come briefly to Albany upon receipt of a formal invitation. On Thursday, December 14, therefore, Anderson sent him a telegram which simply read, "We urge you to come and join the Albany movement." Sherrod and his SNCC companions had had no part in the decision.

King, Abernathy, and Walker arrived late the next day. Their plans were simply to address two mass meetings in the evening, stay overnight, and return to Atlanta in the morning. King made what had become a standard speech for him, but the people of Albany, hearing it for the first time, responded rapturously. Indeed, their intensity surprised King. It reminded him of the first weeks of the Montgomery boycott, he later commented. At the meeting's conclusion Anderson told the crowd that, as no settlement with the city had yet been reached, there would be mass demonstrations the next day. Publicly he asked King to join them. King and his colleagues had neither wanted nor prepared for this. They had been in town only a few hours and had but an imperfect grasp of the local issues and leadership rivalries. Still, King knew he had no choice. To leave town now would be to desert the cause.

At 4 p.m. on Saturday, December 16, King and Anderson led more than 250 marchers toward city hall. After several blocks, Pritchett and his officers barricaded the road and ordered them to disperse or be arrested for parading without a permit. They refused to move and were thus taken into custody, with bond set at $200. King and Anderson refused to make bail, vowing to stay in jail until the city started down the road to desegregation. Abernathy did accept bond so that he could return to Atlanta to rally support for the movement in which SCLC had suddenly and unexpectedly become deeply involved.

The arrests brought tensions in the black community into the open. Those who had opposed King's involvement made public statements emphasizing the movement's local nature and discounting the need for outside support. Yet at the same time Abernathy, back in Atlanta, was making plans for a national pilgrimage of civil rights supporters to Albany. From his jail cell King explained that while he had never intended to do more than make a speech, he was now involved for the duration. He expected to spend Christmas in jail, he said, indeed he promised to do so, and he hoped thousands would join him. Clearly the Albany movement was in danger of unraveling because of these deep internal tensions between those who wished to keep the movement local and those who wished to make Albany a national symbol.

King and Anderson were brought to Albany on Monday for trial. Before the proceedings, the local leadership group announced they had reached verbal agreement with the city on certain issues relating to the arrests, and with vague promises of reform to come. King and Anderson therefore signed their bonds, and despite King's promise they were soon out of jail. King was glad to be out of Albany altogether. Nevertheless, the experience, especially the broken promise, cost him dearly in prestige. Moreover he would have to return to Albany to face trial in the new year.

Albany city officials, however, had no real intention of making any accommodation with the movement, and thus the demonstrations and the arrests continued into 1962. On February 27 King and Abernathy returned to the city to stand trial for their December arrests. After two hours the judge recessed the proceedings, announcing he would reach a verdict within sixty days. King quietly returned to Atlanta as Albany remained unsettled, its white leaders intransigent, its black community deeply divided. The verdict, announced on July 10, was scarcely unexpected. Judge Durden found both King and Abernathy guilty, sentencing them to forty-five days in jail or a fine of $178. Both chose imprisonment—for King a distasteful imperative, given growing SNCC criticism of his seeming unwillingness to put his body on the line, especially after his early release the previous December. Chief Pritchett was deeply unhappy with this development. The Albany movement was sputtering to a halt; King's presence in jail might well revive it. The city's leadership moved quickly. After only two days Pritchett told both prisoners that an "unknown negro" had paid their fines and they were free to go. Unhappily King and Abernathy left, first the jail, and soon the city, knowing that the "unknown negro" did not exist and that the city's white leadership probably secured their release. There seemed little point in remaining after a federal judge issued an order preventing further demonstrations in Albany. King would never defy such an order, and, despite his pledge to remain there till the city capitulated, he soon returned to

Atlanta. Anderson announced that there would be no more mass protests, and that the movement would turn its attention to voter registration.

SCLC's first involvement in a mass action campaign had failed, and King had lost prestige as a result, especially with the young activists of SNCC. But it had taught him some valuable lessons. Albany, located in rural Georgia, and without a moderate white business community inclined to negotiate, was the wrong choice for a mass action campaign. SCLC had involved itself summarily, without careful planning and without understanding the complexities and divisions of the local black community. Chief Pritchett had played a crucial role. By keeping the white mob at bay and by instructing his officers to treat demonstrators gently, even when arresting them, he had successfully prevented the massive disorder that might have provoked federal action. King understood as never before how crucial federal action was to the cause of black freedom. This would never be achieved through changing the hearts and minds of Southern whites, nor through peaceful protests. Legislation was the key, civil rights legislation that would compel the South to treat blacks equally, and this could only come once a national consensus for such action had been created. A far greater crisis than Albany was needed to achieve this, one in which massive white violence would ensure federal intervention. From the ashes of defeat in Albany, then, came the seeds of victory in Birmingham the following year.

The decision to mount a campaign to end segregation in Birmingham, Alabama, was taken at the end of 1962. The reasons were many. King and the SCLC desperately needed a victory to shake off the mounting despair that the Albany debacle had engendered, as well as growing doubts about his personal leadership. Some within his circle now doubted that nonviolence could ever work and were beginning to heed the scoffings of black separatists like Malcolm X. King wanted to push the federal government hard, to force the Kennedys to intervene, and he needed a crisis for that.

Birmingham appeared the ideal venue. Long known as the most thoroughly segregated large city in America, totally unyielding to black demands, and ruled by last-ditch defenders of segregation like Police Commissioner Eugene Theophilus ("Bull") Connor, it was also a city with a mean streak of violence. Blacks had christened it "Bombingham" because of the frequency of racially motivated violence there in the preceding decade. "Bull" Connor and his associates considered the moderation of men like Albany's Pritchett to be fatally weak. They could be counted on to respond ferociously to any attempt to challenge segregation. King and the SCLC had an open invitation from the Reverend Fred Shuttlesworth, head of the Alabama Movement on Human Rights, to conduct demonstrations in Birmingham, thus there was a legitimate reason for moving there. The SCLC therefore decided to conduct a campaign of nonviolent resistance in Birmingham beginning in April 1963, one which, unlike the Albany imbroglio, would be very carefully planned and aimed at provoking confrontation.

The campaign opened on April 3 with the issuing by Shuttlesworth of a manifesto detailing the grievances of Birmingham blacks and calling for rapid progress toward desegregation. At a mass meeting that evening, King vowed he would lead an economic boycott against downtown merchants, accompanied by demonstrations, until "Pharaoh lets God's people go." These boycotts began the next morning and continued for several days. The anticipated arrests excited the attention of the national news media, who were soon flocking to the city, exactly as King had planned. On April 10, trying to counter such unwelcome publicity, city officials obtained a local injunction barring further marches.

King was no longer disposed to obey such local injunctions. Dismissing this one as immoral, he said he would march to city hall on Good Friday, April 12. He made good his word, accompanied by Abernathy, the blind blues singer Al Hibbler, and fifty volunteers, all singing hymns as they approached their destination. Connor, who until now had kept his feelings under control, finally snapped, as King knew he would. He turned the city's fearsome snarling police dogs on the demonstrators as he arrested them, ensuring the television networks a lead story for the evening news.

King spent much of his time in jail composing what has become the classic justification of his nonviolent strategy, "Letter from the Birmingham Jail." Written as a response to eight local ministers who had condemned his campaign as "unwise and untimely," the nineteen-page letter was soon smuggled out of the jail and onto the front pages of most major newspapers. Its reception was overwhelmingly positive, indeed it legitimated the direct-action movement as no other single piece of writing had done.

Couched as usual in the cadences of the Scriptures, and drawing heavily on them for its examples and arguments, the letter was at once an exposition of the evils blacks suffered under segregation, a critique of those who counseled moderation, and a justification of nonviolent direct action as a means of bringing home to white America the urgency of the need to cleanse the nation of racial injustice. Segregation laws degraded human potential, King argued. They tore at the soul and did not conform to the law of God. They were therefore unjust, and one had a moral responsibility to disobey them. That was why he was in Birmingham, to seek justice through civil disobedience. Calling on whites to support him in this, he pointed out that if nonviolence did not work, if integration did not work, then "millions of Negroes, out of frustration and despair, will seek solace and security in black nationalist ideologies, a development that will lead inevitably to a frightening racial nightmare." He concluded by talking about heroes—James Meredith, the women of Montgomery, the students at the sit-ins. "One day the South will know" he said, "that when these disinherited children of God sat down at lunch counters they were in reality standing up for the best in the American dream and the most sacred values in our Judeo-Christian heritage, and thus carrying our whole nation back to great wells of democracy which were dug deep by the founding fathers in the formulation of the Constitution and the Declaration of Independence."

King's letter, influential throughout much of the nation, made no difference to "Bull" Connor and his police, who lost all restraint when confronted with larger demonstrations and more cameras. Movements of support for the marchers arose throughout the country as national tensions grew. Meanwhile King, now out of jail, prepared for the next phase of the campaign.

This began on May 2. That evening, a stunned America watched on national television news the beginning of the "children's crusade." Thousands of Birmingham's black youngsters, some no more than seven years old, marched out of the Sixteenth Street Baptist Church singing freedom songs, chanting slogans, and kneeling in prayer as the police rounded them up and took them to jail. They were completely without fear; this was what made their display so effective. They may also have lacked a full understanding of what they were doing, as King's critics were quick to allege. "Real men," said Malcolm X, did not put babies in the front lines. It did not matter. In Birmingham and throughout the nation, the beginning of the "children's crusade" had decisively altered perceptions of the struggle.

What happened the next day, Friday, May 3, when the children marched again, gave King the confrontation he had deliberately planned for. Connor went completely berserk, ordering police to bar all exits from the church, trapping about half the youngsters inside. Those who escaped ran to a nearby park, pursued by Connor, his dogs, and a new and deadly weapon, high-pressure fire hoses. Adults and children alike were clubbed, menaced by the dogs, and doused by jets of water sufficiently powerful to tear the bark from trees. The water tore the clothes from their backs, cut their skins, and swept them back into the streets. Hundreds more were arrested that day and the next, but it was the scenes from the Friday attack that most jolted the nation. The snarling dogs, the water hoses knocking young and old alike off their feet, the savage beatings, all there on the nightly news, did more than anything else to create the consensus that would make federal action not only possible but mandatory.

Still the Kennedys were slow to move. Like everyone else, they publicly deplored the violence and looked for the restoration of peace in the city, but the president feared the political consequences of federal intervention. Talks began between the SCLC leaders and a group of moderate Birmingham businessmen, but progress was slow and the demonstrations continued. The violence escalated as the police responded predictably. Connor, goaded beyond endurance at the blacks' seeming lack of fear, exulted at the mayhem. Some blacks now began to fight back with bottles and bricks. A bloodbath seemed only a matter of time, and the local talks reached a new level of urgency, as did the national clamor for presidential intervention. On May 10 an accord was announced, "the climax," said King, "of a long struggle for justice, freedom and human dignity in the city of Birmingham." Lunch counters, rest rooms, and drinking fountains were to be desegregated, and discriminatory hiring practices would be abolished according to an agreed timetable. It was, King claimed, "the most magnificent victory for justice we've ever seen in the Deep South."

For Connor, for other local and state officials, for the White Citizens Council, for the Klan, and for thousands of Birmingham's white citizens, it was a betrayal, and they vowed vengeance. Bombs exploded in black districts that evening, and angry crowds gathered. The Birmingham ghetto surged with violence and hatred, an angry harbinger of things to come, despite the best efforts of Walker and other SCLC officials to contain it. King's presence the next day helped calm things, and the desegregation pact was quickly implemented. Order at last returned to the city.

The Birmingham struggle inspired blacks across the nation. If a regime like Connor's could be defeated, what city administration could withstand the power of an aroused people? There would be "little Birminghams" throughout the United States that summer of 1963, as the nature of black protest changed. There would be no more tokenism; "Freedom Now" was the cry, freedom in every aspect. Birmingham had stimulated, in the words of James Farmer of the Congress of Racial Equality (CORE), "a spiritual emancipation," a freedom from fear, a new pride and assertiveness. In one short year King had put behind him the failure of Albany, effectively buried by the triumph that was Birmingham.

Martin Luther King wrote that "the sound of the explosion in Birmingham reached all the way to Washington." In this he was surely correct. The main consequence of the summer of 1963 was John F. Kennedy's realization that the federal government could no longer hang back, that he too must embrace the civil rights movement. His own personal morality partly dictated this shift, so did his sense of what was now politically possible. He signaled this new direction on June 11, 1963, in the most important television speech he ever made on a domestic issue, a speech his advisers had warned him not to give. Calling the issue of racial justice "a moral issue . . . as old as the Scriptures and . . . as clear as the American Constitution," he spoke intensely of the discrimination under which black Americans lived. The time for delay had long gone, the president said. "This nation, for all its hopes and all its boasts, will not be fully free until all its citizens are free," and it was time for Congress to legislate this freedom. A week later Kennedy sent to the legislators the most comprehensive civil rights bill in American history. It aimed to desegregate public accommodations, greatly increase the pace of school desegregation, provide for federal registrars to enroll black voters, improve the general economic status of blacks, and empower the government to withhold funds from federally financed facilities that discriminated against blacks. Hailed by most black organizations and by the white liberal community as an act—no matter how belated—of courageous leadership, the president's proposal meant the cutting of political ties with the South. It was, said an outraged Senator Eastland, "a complete blueprint for a totalitarian state."

In order to swell support for Kennedy's legislation, King and the SCLC leadership began to prepare for a March on Washington in August 1963. The idea itself was not new. A. Philip Randolph of the Brotherhood of Sleeping Car Porters had proposed such a march in 1941, when defense industry jobs had been denied blacks. Now, with King, the veteran leader revived his plan, this time to capture the national imagination by appealing to those same ideals that the president had referred to so eloquently in his June 11 speech. The

Kennedys, however, were not enthusiastic about the proposal, fearing violence. So did some more moderate black leaders like Roy Wilkins of the NAACP. King, Randolph, and James Farmer stood firm, and the president acquiesced. At his press conference on July 17 he even referred to the march, now certain to take place, as being in the great American tradition of peaceful assembly.

On August 28, 1963, nearly 250,000 demonstrators, black and white, marched peacefully in the nation's capital to petition for black rights. There was not a hint of violence; indeed, the day became a celebration—"a jubilation," Ralph Abernathy later called it. The crowd sang along with Joan Baez, Bob Dylan, Peter, Paul and Mary, Odetta, and Mahalia Jackson. The day was hot and humid, the speeches long and sometimes boring, but the assemblage listened patiently to them all. There was nothing boring, however, about Martin Luther King's address, the final one for the afternoon. As he spoke of his dream, of a nation united in social and racial justice, the crowd was uplifted with the emotion of the moment. "I have a dream," he cried, "that one day on the red hills of Georgia the sons of former slaves and the sons of former slaveowners will be able to sit down together at the table of brotherhood."

> I have a dream that my four little children will one day live in a nation where they will not be judged by the color of their skin but the content of their character. I have a dream today. . . .
>
> Let freedom ring . . . when we let it ring from every village and every hamlet, from every state and every city, we will be able to speed up the day when all God's children, black men and white men, Jews and Gentiles, Protestants and Catholics, will be able to join hands and sing in the words of that old Negro spiritual, "Free at last! Free at last! Thank God almighty, we are free at last."

The day was a stirring triumph for King. He had transformed a meandering march into one of America's historic events. He had touched the hearts of millions. He had made eventual passage of the civil rights bill more certain. More than that, he had during 1963 made himself the leader of America's black citizens, the most effective proponent of the integrationist ideal. His philosophy of nonviolence seemed to have triumphed: an end to segregation was at hand. He had delivered, as he said he would. For the time being, the angry tones of violence had been quelled by his prophetic vision. He had, in fact, moved a nation.

4

"Sitting-in for Justice, Riding for Freedom"

ON JANUARY 31, 1960, Joseph McNeill, a freshman at North Carolina's all-black Agricultural and Technical College in Greensboro, asked for a hamburger at the diner in the town's bus terminal. "We don't serve Negroes here," was the waitress's predictable reply, for almost all restaurants in the South were segregated, either by custom, state statute, or local ordinance. That night, back in the college dormitory, McNeill talked about the incident with his roommate, Ezell Blair, and close friends Franklin McCain and David Richmond. The young men spent most of their free time together. Three of them, in fact, had grown up in Greensboro and had attended the same secondary school, Dudley High. They had, as William Chafe observed, "come of age, intellectually and politically, in the years since the *Brown* decision," and were deeply resentful at how little had happened since then. Waiting for court action to secure their rights took far too long, of that they were convinced. They had often talked of taking action themselves, to speed the process. That night they agreed to do just that the next day. In this decision they moved the civil rights movement into a new phase of activity.

The four young men had been deeply influenced by the events of Montgomery and by Martin Luther King's subsequent writings and speeches. But they were not connected to the SCLC in any way. What they did was spontaneous, without script or direction. King so came to dominate the civil rights movement, and later historians' assessments of it, that it is sometimes hard to realize that many activities in the early 1960s occurred beyond his ambit of influence. Sometimes they were the result of spontaneous action; more commonly they were planned by agencies over which King had no control and with whom his relations were sometimes uneasy.

The next day the four young men went shopping at the downtown Greensboro Woolworth's. They bought toothpaste and other personal items, then sat at the lunch counter, ordering coffee and doughnuts. "We don't serve colored," said the waitress. "Yes, you do," responded Blair, displaying his receipts of the items he had just purchased. The waitress quickly called the manager. Politely he asked them to leave; equally politely they refused. They would go only after they had eaten, Blair explained. By this time they had attracted a crowd, predominantly white and overwhelmingly abusive, scarcely surprising to the students. What did surprise them, however, was the reaction of one middle-aged white woman. She made a point of patting them all on the back as she left the store. "Ah, you should have done it two years ago," she said. "It's a good thing I think you're doing." "Scared as hell," the four young men left only when the store closed, vowing to return the next day. The "sit-in" movement, a new phase of the civil rights struggle, had begun.

The four men returned the next day, after a meeting the previous evening at which they called for volunteers to help them. They also pledged themselves to passive resistance in the King model. They would never fight back, they said, never abuse those who abused them. Their movement, like the Montgomery boycott, would be nonviolent and imbued with the spirit of Christian love. All the original four protesters were deeply committed, churchgoing Christians.

Twenty-three A & T students came with them the next day, together with four black women from nearby Bennett College. On Wednesday, February 3, the number had swollen to sixty-three, almost filling the lunch counter. On Thursday the first whites joined them—three young women from the Woman's College of the University of North Carolina's Greensboro campus. Now there were so many blacks that they overflowed Woolworth's, and some sat in at the nearby Kress store as well. By the end of the week city officials deemed it time to negotiate, and meanwhile the demonstrations ceased.

As was usually the case it turned out that the city officials were not serious; they simply wanted to stop the sit-ins, fundamentally misjudging (as whites were to do throughout the South) the strength of the black commitment. Thus they fudged and dissembled, and in the end made it clear there would be no real change in Greensboro. The demonstrations therefore recommenced on April 1 and continued daily. On April 2 city officials made a fatal mistake, arresting forty-five students for trespassing. Enraged, the Greensboro black community now joined in, boycotting selected city stores. Profits fell away, and this brought the white power structure seriously to the bargaining table. Just six months after the four students had first defied Southern custom, blacks could now be served at all the city's lunch counters. It had been a swift and relatively painless victory.

Although public accommodations in the South would not be fully integrated until after the passage of the Civil Rights Act of 1964, of all the tactics used during those years it was the sit-in that brought the most immediate results. One reason was the demeanor of the demonstrators themselves. Well dressed, polite, never menacing or retaliatory, they provided a contrast to the whites who abused them that even impressed their most bitter opponents. Wrote the segregationist editor, James K. Kilpatrick, in the *Richmond News Leader*, commenting on the Greensboro events, "Here were the colored students, in coats, white shirts, ties, and one of them was reading Goethe and one was taking notes from a biology text. And here, on the sidewalk outside, was a gang of white boys come to heckle, a ragtail rabble, slack-jawed, black-jacketed, grinning fit to kill. . . . Eheu! It gives one pause."

All over the South in 1960, students, inspired by the example of the Greensboro four, sat-in. In North Carolina, within a week of the first Greensboro demonstration, sit-ins had spread to Raleigh, Durham, High Point, and Winston-Salem before fanning out across the region. By April 1960 more than two thousand students had been arrested in seventy-eight Southern cities and towns; by September 1961, according to the Southern Regional Council, more than seventy thousand blacks and whites had actively participated in sit-ins. They were often successful, as the Greensboro activists had been. By August 1960, twenty-eight Southern cities had desegregated their lunch counters, and a few had even done the same with theaters and restaurants.

Not all of the sit-ins had been as relatively violence-free as the one in Greensboro; indeed, violence became the normal white response. In Portsmouth, Virginia, police loosed their dogs on demonstrators, while in Tallahassee arrested students decided to serve significant jail sentences rather than pay their fines, thus introducing a new weapon, the "jail-in," to the demonstrators' armory. The sit-ins in Nashville, Tennessee, led by students from Fisk University with the help of a few whites from Vanderbilt, turned especially ugly as the police gave white hecklers free rein. Day after day students were cursed at, beaten, and kicked. Young women were burned with cigarette butts, and hundreds were arrested and jailed. As with Greensboro, however, the city's black community provided support by boycotting downtown stores, a particularly effective tactic during the Easter shopping season. In response, Nashville Mayor Ben West at first tried palliative measures, proposing, on advice from a specially appointed committee, that only half of each lunch counter be integrated, and half remain reserved for whites. The students would have none of such tokenism, so the sit-ins and marches continued, the violence escalated, and, after further negotiations, desegregation of downtown facilities came to Nashville. In the course of the conflict, Mayor West searched his soul and concluded, as he told student leader Diane Nash, that it was morally wrong to sell people goods in a store and yet not permit them to eat there. For a few whites like West, the sit-in movement presented the moral dimension of the civil rights struggle as nothing had done previously.

The most comprehensive sit-in campaign took place in Atlanta. There an aspiring young poet and Morehouse College student, Julian Bond, son of the noted black educator Horace Mann Bond, was galvanized into action by Lonnie King, a former soldier and current college football hero. Together they led a campaign calling not only for the desegregation of lunch counters but of all public facilities, voting rights for blacks, and equality in employment and educational opportunity. Bond and King decided to use the sit-in as the campaign's main strategic weapon. Throughout the year this battle was fought, city leaders, as always, tried tokenism, which, as always, the young activists rejected. By the end of the year Atlanta's large and influential black community had been won over. Some sat-in with the students, most simply boycotted the downtown stores. Not until 1961 did the white power structure crack, finally admitting that the pressure had become too great. On September 27 desegregation came to Atlanta, and Julian Bond had put behind him forever his dream of a poet's career.

The sit-in movement radicalized the generation of students who, like the Greensboro four, had grown to political consciousness in the years since the *Brown* decision. Deeply influenced by King's example and writings, drawn to his nonviolent philosophical stance, they had become thoroughly disenchanted with the glacial pace of change since 1954. From the perspective of the late 1990s, the right to eat a hamburger in a downtown store may not seem terribly important, but to these young people nothing epitomized their second-class status or emphasized their "difference" more than their inability to do so. They had no plans to win that right through the court system; it would take far too long. In 1960 they decided to take it themselves. In so doing, the students quickened the pace of racial change, spurred the adult black community into support and action, and made Southern whites realize they were sitting on a time bomb. The sit-ins and the consequent boycotts could not be written off by whites as the work of outside agitators like King, or nefarious Communists. The people involved were local people, people they knew. After the sit-ins, few whites bothered to talk about the contented status of "their blacks" anymore. They knew it wasn't true. If they continued to defend white supremacy—and most did—it was from a much more realistic perspective.

Finally, the sit-in movement changed the image young black men and women had of themselves. Like those who walked Montgomery's streets, they had taken on the power structure and won, and they believed they could go on winning. Perhaps the most important consequence of this new positive spirit was the attempt to institutionalize it in what was to become a key agency for change, the Student Nonviolent Coordinating Committee. Formed in April 1960, in the euphoric first flush of sit-in success, and with Ella Baker as its midwife, the early SNCC perfectly epitomized this confident, impatient, even naive spirit. Baker knew there were much harder struggles ahead than those over lunch counters. In her opening address to the student delegates, "More Than a Hamburger," Baker stressed this point, urging the students to keep going, to use the momentum of the sit-ins to work toward changing the whole society, not just its lunch counters. King also spoke, reminding them that nonviolence was a whole way of being, not simply a tactic.

Most of the students had trouble with this. They rather agreed with James Lawson, another speaker, that while nonviolence was well suited to the present situation, it might not always be so, and that increased militancy might one day be necessary. Nevertheless the conference ended with the spirit of King's beloved community everywhere in evidence, and with a decision to form a permanent, independent organization to coordinate future activities, one that would work closely with SCLC but remain independent of it. SNCC was thus born out of boundless optimism, righteousness, and faith in America, all qualities which the organization would lose over the years.

The next stage of the civil rights struggle also involved young people. This was the "Freedom Ride" movement of 1961. The story of Wilson Head's journey through the South in 1946, with which this book opened, was an account of one man's attempt to test the recent Supreme Court decision invalidating segregation in interstate travel. The following year a more serious attempt was made by representatives of the

Congress of Racial Equality (CORE). James Farmer and Bayard Rustin had established CORE in 1942. Its philosophy, which set it apart from the NAACP, was always to confront racial discrimination by nonviolent direct action. Indeed it was CORE that had pioneered the sit-in, not in the South but in Chicago and the border cities of St. Louis and Baltimore. In 1947 CORE had agreed to sponsor members of the New York–based, socialist-leaning Fellowship of Reconciliation, including Rustin, who planned to ride interstate buses and trains in the upper South, again to test the court decision. The interracial group set out from Washington on April 9, some by train, with Kentucky as the final destination, others by bus. Those on the bus got only as far as Chapel Hill, North Carolina. When they refused to move to the rear seats after being told to do so, they were arrested, found guilty of violating North Carolina's segregation laws, and sentenced to thirty days' jail on the ground that as they had planned to travel only to Greensboro, they were involved in intrastate, not interstate, commerce. The decision was upheld on appeal, and the riders, including Rustin, spent thirty days on a road gang. This particular journey received no publicity or press attention, and it changed Southern practices not a whit. Yet it did provide a model for the future, one which CORE would reinvent in 1961, in the next decisive phase of the civil rights movement.

In 1960 the Supreme Court had extended its prohibition against segregation in vehicles engaged in interstate travel so as to include terminal facilities as well. CORE's director, James Farmer, decided therefore that the times were propitious for another "Freedom Ride." CORE's intention, as Farmer put it, "was to provoke the Southern authorities into arresting us and thereby prod the Justice Department into enforcing the law of the land." The aim was to bring on confrontation, and with it, national publicity. CORE was, as Farmer admitted, "counting on the bigots of the South to do our work for us."

As in the 1947 ride, Farmer planned to use interracial groups. But in 1961 they would be testing not only seating arrangements but also terminal restaurants, waiting rooms, and rest rooms. Moreover, the riders would not confine themselves to the upper South. And they pledged, if arrested, to go to jail rather than pay fines. In late April, Farmer wrote to the president, to the bus companies, and to the FBI, preparing them for the project. No one replied.

On May 4 seven blacks and six whites, divided into two groups, left Washington on Trailways and Greyhound buses. The blacks were all veterans of the previous year's sit-ins; the whites were from peace groups. Slowly they traveled through Virginia and North Carolina without problems. Not until the Greyhound group reached Rock Hill, South Carolina, did the first violence occur. There local hoodlums beat up John Lewis, one of the black riders, as he tried to enter the waiting room. Although the police were present, they made no attempt to prevent the beating, but they did, in the end, allow the riders to enter the waiting room. Both buses then proceeded to Atlanta, where the travelers spent a rest day before continuing the journey, through Alabama, to Jackson, Mississippi.

On May 14 the Greyhound bus departed first. When it reached Anniston, Alabama, it was met by an angry mob armed with clubs and iron bars, who proceeded to break the bus's windows and slash its tires. The bus left Anniston under police protection, the mob chasing it in cars. Six miles out of town they halted it, threw a bomb through the window, and then barred the doors. The riders escaped just before the bus exploded and burned, and were set upon by the mob. Fortunately help was at hand in the tough person of the Reverend

Fred Shuttlesworth and a large group of supporters who took the shocked and injured riders to Birmingham. A mob set upon the Trailways riders, too, when they arrived in Anniston, but it was in Birmingham where they struck the worst violence yet encountered. There, though an angry crowd had been gathering all day and trouble was inevitable, no police were in sight when the bus pulled in. Not until the crowd had thoroughly worked the riders over, seriously injuring one of them, did the officers arrive. Still, those physically able to do so wished to continue the journey, traveling to Montgomery as a single unit. Neither Trailways nor Greyhound would accept them. Reluctantly they flew to New Orleans, courtesy of the Justice Department. The CORE-sponsored Freedom Ride had ended.

SNCC leaders, however, insisted that the journey must continue, even with different people on board, in order to deny the racists their victory. Twenty-one activists from Atlanta and Nashville thus traveled to Birmingham, planning to make the next leg to Montgomery. After considerable harassment and delay, because at first no driver would take them, they finally left on the morning of May 20. The two-hour journey went without incident, for they were accompanied by police cars and helicopters. It was different, however, when they reached Montgomery's city limits. All the police disappeared, John Lewis, who had stayed with the group, recalled. When they reached the bus terminal, all was quiet, unnaturally so. Warily they alighted, and then it happened—"people just started pouring out of the station, out of the buildings, from all over the place." Justice Department officials, sent there by Robert Kennedy, could not believe their eyes. There was no police presence at all, one official reported to the attorney general. The mob, estimated at one thousand people, had free rein, and the riders were brutally beaten. John Lewis was knocked unconscious. A white rider, Jim Zwerg, suffered severe spinal injuries. Even two white women were not spared. By the time the police arrived, all the riders needed hospitalization, as did President Kennedy's emissary to Alabama's governor, felled by an iron bar while trying to help the white women. Montgomery's police commissioner explained his lack of action thus: "We have no intention of standing guard for a bunch of troublemakers coming into our city."

The carnage at Montgomery made international news, thus fulfilling the ride's original purpose. James Farmer had his riot, though he was not there to see it. Reluctantly the Kennedys decided that it was time to act, that they could no longer tolerate the defiance of federal law nor the damage it was doing to America's international image—though they were angry at the Freedom Riders for, as they saw it, provoking the conflict. After calling on Alabama officials to keep the peace, the attorney general announced that a force of four hundred federal marshals would be sent to the state to help them do so.

Martin Luther King was also reluctantly drawn into the conflict. Although not initially consulted by CORE, he had been kept abreast of events. After the Montgomery imbroglio, he agreed to address a mass rally at Ralph Abernathy's church, supporting the ride's continuation. On May 21 twelve hundred men, women, and children crammed into the church while across the street a crowd of angry whites gathered in a local park. Again the police were absent, and the crowd grew ugly, hurling firebombs at the church and coming very close to bursting into it. Fortunately Kennedy's federal marshals arrived in time, ringing the church to prevent further violence. Belatedly Governor Patterson ordered the National Guard and state troopers to help them, and the angry crowd dispersed, but it had been a very close call.

The next day King, now very much part of the action, James Farmer, and the student leaders, disregarding Robert Kennedy's plea for a cooling-off period, announced that the Freedom Ride would continue. More volunteers came to Montgomery in response, and on May 24 a group of twenty-seven, some newly arrived, some bearing the bruises and cuts of earlier encounters, left for Jackson, Mississippi. Troopers guarded them every inch of the way, yet the riders were apprehensive about what would happen once they reached Mississippi's capital. James Farmer, who, unlike King, had not been able to resist the pressure to join the riders, recalled that as they reached the city's outskirts they all started to sing. "Hallelujah, I'm traveling," they sang,

Hallelujah, ain't it fine
Hallelujah, I'm traveling
Down Jackson's main line.

There was to be no violence, however, for Robert Kennedy had made a deal with Mississippi's racist Senator James Eastland. If the mobs were kept away, the federal government would do nothing to prevent the riders' immediate arrests. And this is what happened. They stepped off the bus at Jackson and were immediately arrested and taken to jail. There they stayed rather than pay their fines, as others joined them. That summer three hundred were jailed in Jackson alone, and more than a thousand whites and blacks, young and old, Northerners and Southerners, took part in Freedom Rides. They created the intended crisis, and in the end they forced the government to act. On September 22 the Interstate Commerce Commission issued rules not only making it mandatory that all interstate carriers and terminals display signs stating that seating was "without regard to race, color, creed and national origin," but also banning such carriers from using terminals that refused to comply. The battle of interstate travel was over. The Supreme Court ruling of 1946 would finally be enforced.

The Freedom Rides campaign produced several important results. First, it gave CORE a real boost. Henceforth CORE became a major player in the civil rights struggle, challenging King, the SCLC, the NAACP, and even SNCC for leadership of the fight. Second, the rides showed again that victories could be won, even in the Deep South, provided the federal government could be brought into the action, and this could best be achieved by provoking confrontation. Third, even more than the sit-ins or the struggle at Little Rock, the rides showed the violent side of Southern racism to the nation and the world. The brutality of the mobs and the passive support of white law-enforcement officers disgusted millions and won many to the civil rights cause. For those who were beaten or who went to jail, the experience was profound. It made them even more skeptical of King's optimism, and in particular his vision of a beloved community. Whites were not about to change, the protesters were coming to understand. Love would not conquer all. Rather, power, the power of the federal government, wielded on their behalf, was what would bring real change. But how were they to enlist it?

For many of the young men and women of SNCC, their commitment deepened by the sit-ins and the Freedom Rides, part-time involvement in the struggle was no longer enough. The fight from now on would demand their total existence. Thus they left their homes and their colleges to work full-time for the movement and at the grassroots, interacting with local people in small communities, often in situations of continuous danger, trying to change the lives of those they now lived with. In so doing they moved the civil rights struggle into the next phase.

The Freedom Rides thoroughly shook the Kennedy administration, and certainly both the president and his brother were keen to avoid further violence. Yet they recognized that pressure for change could not be stopped. Their job therefore became to divert it, if they could, down less confrontational paths. It was to this end that Robert Kennedy met with student leaders on June 16, 1961. He urged them to concentrate their future energies on voter registration projects rather than on more direct-action activities. The attorney general and his Justice Department aides argued that the key to Southern change was the vote, that the major philanthropic organizations were much more likely to provide funding for voter registration than for more confrontationist schemes—always a consideration for the financially strapped SNCC—and that they could count on FBI protection if they followed that course. The students were suspicious of the government's motives, though some admitted the cogency of the argument. Without the vote, and the consequent ability to influence local power in the South, lasting change was unlikely. Reconstruction had proved that.

James Forman, SNCC's executive director, eventually convinced his troops that there was no real dichotomy between voter registration and direct-action programs. To persuade Black Belt residents to swallow their fear and march to the courthouse in an effort to register would effectively combine the two. The white reaction was sure to be extreme, so there would be more than enough violence to attract national publicity. By October SNCC had agreed to join with the NAACP, SCLC, and CORE in a Voter Education Project funded by the major foundations and administered by the Southern Regional Council. It was to run for two and a half years, from April 1962. SNCC was to be responsible for Alabama and

Mississippi, because, as one worker wryly recalled, "nobody else wanted 'em."

SNCC's campaign began in the Mississippi Delta and initially drew heavily on the experience of Robert Moses, who had been working on his own in McComb, Mississippi, since 1961. Moses, a native New Yorker with a degree in philosophy from Harvard, had already suffered severe beatings directly resulting from his work. He was thus well able to explain to the SNCC workers just how difficult and dangerous was their task, and how small would be the measure of victory. Yet there was never any question in his mind of giving up. Moses's cool bravery, his persistence, his defiance of white authority marked him as an authentic hero. The SNCC activists also linked up with some of the most courageous of all the fighters for civil rights. These were the local community leaders, men like Amzie Moore, head of the NAACP in Mississippi's Cleveland County, who, at great personal danger, first persuaded the local communities to accept the outsiders, and then worked with them. Often veterans of a struggle that had shaped their whole lives, they provided, in the historian Adam Fairclough's words, "the strong base, the bedrock, of the civil rights movement." In Louisiana, where the volunteers labored under CORE rather than SNCC direction, they found local people similarly dedicated to helping them, people like Bill Harleaux of Iberville Parish, a World War II veteran who had been an activist for twenty years. In West Feliciana Parish, where no blacks had voted since 1922, two elderly women provided the workers with food and shelter while one of them allowed her home to be used for voter education clinics. For the workers, the very presence of such people was inspiring, and their local knowledge was invaluable. Years later, veterans of the movement still recalled working with these local activists as the most positive aspect of their civil rights experience.

The first SNCC Voter Registration School opened in Pike County, Mississippi, on August 7, 1962. A few days later its first "graduates" attempted to register there. They were refused, and one of them was shot. Undaunted, Robert Moses persuaded three Smith County blacks to try to register at the county seat in Liberty. Again they were deemed unqualified, and Moses soon found himself beaten and in jail. Later, in Liberty, Moses and Travis Britt, a student from New York, were savagely beaten by a mob as they accompanied four blacks to the registrar's office—punishment, the whites said, for thinking they "could come down here and teach people how to vote." A fortnight later, Herbert Lee, a local farmer who had been helping Moses, was shot dead by a Mississippi state representative after an argument. His assailant was never charged, but no one was left in any doubt as to the reason for Lee's death. The violence with which white Mississippians resisted this first attempt to secure for Mississippi's blacks the political rights guaranteed all citizens profoundly shocked the SNCC workers. It also made a mockery of Robert Kennedy's insistence that such activity was unlikely to produce the violent responses the direct-action campaigns had provoked.

In Louisiana the CORE workers experienced similar violence and intimidation. James Farmer missed the March on Washington in August 1963. He was in jail in Ascension Parish, having led a voter registration march there. A rally in his support was forcibly broken up by police, who used fire hoses and tear gas on the demonstrators, as well as their trusted billy clubs. Mimi Feingold, a white worker, recalled seeing injured women "kicking and screaming in pain" after the assault. Farmer, released from jail, had to escape to New

Orleans in the back of a hearse. Not only the Delta Project workers lived in a world of violence and constant apprehension.

Still, the danger was greatest, the violence most uncontrolled in Mississippi. What had happened to Robert Moses in the first months of the campaign became the way of life for SNCC workers. They lived in daily fear for their safety, in an environment unremittingly hostile, protected neither by the local police, which was no surprise, nor by the Department of Justice, which was. But they kept on, holding classes, accompanying people to the registrar's office, never knowing what would happen to them but always aware that their chances of succeeding, of getting even one new voter on the rolls, were exceedingly slight. Living in such constant tension took its toll on their mental and physical health. It also changed them as people. It did not take too long before most of them had lost any lingering commitment to Martin Luther King's beloved community. They had suffered too much at white hands, had watched whites pervert the law to prevent black registration, had been beaten by white police officers, jailed by white sheriffs, and convicted by white judges—all for trying to help people exercise their basic rights of citizenship. The notion of an integrated society where color did not matter, a society fashioned through redemptive love, seemed ludicrous in the light of their recent experience. The violence done to them made King's nonviolent philosophy seem similarly unrealistic. If they remained nonviolent themselves, it was not as an ideal but purely as a tactic, a recognition that in the Mississippi Delta to fight back would surely bring destruction. Finally, their experiences, the way institutions were used against them, made them question the very bedrock of American democracy itself. Martin Luther King might continue, publicly at least, to proclaim his faith in the decency of American government and the institutions that underpinned it. Working in the rural South as they were, the SNCC volunteers found it increasingly difficult to share his dream.

What, then, kept them going? Without doubt the strength, commitment, and conviction of the local people they worked with. To go to the courthouse was not only to suffer ridicule and intimidation, it was also to risk precarious economic livelihood. Black tenants who tried to register often lost their land, farmers their bank credit or their supplies from the local store. They were denied welfare, and there was always the prospect of a beating—or worse. Yet they supported the civil rights workers desperately. Some even became activists themselves. Take the well-known example of Mrs. Fanny Lou Hamer, sharecropper, of Ruleville, Mississippi, later to become a leader in the Mississippi movement. Recalling the first time SNCC workers came in secret to her place, she said:

> Nobody ever came out into the country and talked to real farmers and things because this is the next thing this country has done: it divided us into classes, and if you hadn't arrived at a certain level, you wasn't treated no better by blacks than you was by the whites. And it was these kids who broke a lot of that down. They treated us like we were special and we loved 'em. . . . We didn't feel uneasy about our language might not be right or something. We just felt we could talk to 'em. We trusted 'em.

Mrs. Hamer listened closely to what the SNCC workers were saying and, inspired by the message, presented herself at the registrar's office in Indianola, Mississippi, on August 1, 1962. That night she was ordered to leave her land and never to be seen there again. Radicalized by the experience, she went to work full-time for the Voter Education Project. For that, when returning from a workshop in South Carolina on June

9, 1963, she and eight other women were taken from a bus in Winona, Mississippi, and so severely beaten by police that she never fully recovered. Yet her commitment never wavered. It was people like her, local people, from whom the SNCC workers drew continued strength and inspiration.

Until 1963 the young workers were overwhelmingly black. In the fall of that year, however, a number of white students, mostly recruited by the liberal activist Allard Lowenstein, came down to help. There was to be a state gubernatorial election that year, and since blacks were barred from the political process, the SNCC leadership, now working with the SCLC and the NAACP in a loose federation called the Council of Federated Organizations (COFO), decided to hold a parallel election to show that Mississippi's blacks wanted a part in the state's politics. For two weeks white college students worked alongside blacks, helping with the "freedom campaign." Although there was tension between the youngsters and the SNCC veterans, on the whole the experience was positive. And for the first time the FBI provided some protection for the project workers—they were, after all, the sons and daughters of the white establishment. Perhaps, thought Robert Moses, cynical as it sounded, this might be the way ahead: greater involvement with whites. The Justice Department had left the black volunteers to their fate, despite the attorney general's initial assurances of protection. Perhaps the government would not be so casual if young whites were at risk. The presence of whites might also focus the attention of the media, especially the television networks, on the Magnolia State.

Certainly SNCC activity there needed a boost. The workers were tired, worn down by the pervasive climate of fear. "It was always there," wrote one of them, Cleveland Sellers, "always stretched like a tight steel wire between the pit of the stomach and the center of the brain." They knew that in terms of raising significantly the number of registered black voters in the state, they had failed. In two years the proportion had risen only 1.4 percent from 5.3 percent to 6.7 percent. The other civil rights bodies, in particular the NAACP, were by now barely cooperative, and the Voter Education Project leaders had decided to spend no more money in the state. All they had done, SNCC worker Lawrence Guyot bitterly admitted, was to raise the level of death. Sixty-three blacks, he estimated, had been murdered in the state as a result of the campaign, and nothing had been done about the killings. It is scarcely surprising that in their despair, facing the brutal intransigence of the white power structure, and in their utter disillusionment with the federal government's failure to protect them, some began at last to listen to new and angry voices, positing very different outcomes to the national travail over race than the liberal ideal of Martin Luther King.

Malcolm X, originally from Detroit, was in his youth a small-time Harlem criminal and numbers runner. Sent to prison in 1946 at the age of twenty-one, it was there he first encountered black separatism in the Nation of Islam, or Black Muslims as they were commonly called. Converted to their cause while in jail, he became, on his parole in 1952, a Muslim minister and a protégé of the Nation's leader, Elijah Muhammad. By 1960 he had become a hero in the Harlem ghetto and to thousands of blacks throughout the North because of his articulately delivered message of hate and pride—hate for white America, pride for blacks everywhere. Blacks found themselves in a caste situation, he said, for no other reason than white racism. Blacks were not the source of their problems, whites were. For the young blacks of the ghetto, full of anger and pain, this was liberating stuff indeed.

By the end of 1963 some Southern blacks were beginning to heed Malcolm's message. No one was more dismissive of the civil rights movement, more contemptuous of the goal of racial integration than he. King's message of redemption through love was more than just mistaken, Malcolm said, it was puerile, ignoring as it did the realities of power in America, the utter corruption of the system. "Whoever heard of angry revolutionists all harmonizing We Shall Overcome . . . Suum Day," was his withering dismissal of the 1963 Washington march, "while tripping and swaying along arm-in-arm with the very people they were supposed to be angrily revolting against? Whoever heard of angry revolutionists swinging their bare feet together with their oppressor in lily-pad park pools, with gospels and guitars and I Have a Dream speeches?" Integration with whites, as an ideal, was self-defeating. It simply continued the enemy in power. The future for the black man was a separatist one, apart from whites. Either he returned to Africa or occupied and controlled separate territory and institutions within the United States.

Malcolm similarly dismissed nonviolence. "If someone puts a hand on you," he urged, "send him to the cemetery." Nonviolence would never win black freedom. Force, the force of racism, might well have to be met with force, the force of freedom. Blacks had to fight racism "by any means necessary," he insisted. "The day of nonviolent resistance is over." "Revolutions are never based upon love-your-enemy," he said in early 1964, "and-pray-for-those-who-despitefully-use-you. And revolutions are never waged singing 'We shall overcome.' Revolutions are based on bloodshed."

Initially Malcolm X's message had little appeal for Southern blacks, not even for those most active in the freedom struggle. Themselves products of a deeply Christian culture, reinforced by the strength of King's biblical rhetoric and profoundly Christian ideology, and sharing his vision of the beloved community, the hate-filled tones of the ghetto seemed both threatening and culturally alien. Two years of life in rural Mississippi, Georgia, or Louisiana, however, two years of fighting white power, two years of experiencing white brutality had certainly had its effect. By the end of 1963 a significant number of SNCC workers were willing to concede that Malcolm may have a point.

Bob Moses, however, was not yet ready to make that concession. He still believed in the vital importance of gaining the ballot as the key to achieving local power. Despite the withdrawal of Voter Education Project funds, he and his field director, David Dennis, planned a massive voter registration drive for Mississippi in 1964. Drawing on the experience of the previous year, they proposed to invite hundreds of white college students to help them, mainly to focus sufficient national attention on the state so as to place voting rights firmly on the political agenda. "We knew that if we had brought in a thousand blacks," Dennis recalled, "the country would have watched them slaughtered without doing anything about it. Bring in a thousand whites and the country is going to react to that." Thus was "Freedom Summer" born.

In mid-June hundreds of student volunteers for the Mississippi Summer Project, again mainly the children of the affluent middle classes, gathered for training in Oxford, Ohio. There they received only the most cursory of briefings before traveling south to the rural hamlets and small towns of Mississippi. They did the best they could, but the gulf between their optimism, their cultural assumptions, and their life experiences, and the worldview of the rural blacks they had come to help, was frequently impassable.

Freedom Summer had hardly begun before the event that would dominate national attention occurred. Three workers were reported missing near Philadelphia, Mississippi, in Neshoba County. Michael Schwerner was a twenty-four-year-old New York social worker who had been running a CORE project in Meridian since January with his wife, Rita. Andrew Goodman was only twenty-one; also from New York and a student at Queens College, he was a Summer Project volunteer. James Chaney, a black Mississippian, also twenty-one, had been working for the CORE project as a volunteer. The three had come to Neshoba County to inspect the ruins of a black church recently destroyed by Klansmen, and to show solidarity with the black community there. On the way back to Meridian, having just passed through Philadelphia, they were arrested by the town's deputy sheriff, Cecil Price, on a trumped-up speeding charge. They were never seen alive again—except by their murderers.

What happened after their arrest is now known through the testimony of paid Klan informers at federal trials. Released after dark, the three young men were escorted to a deserted road where three carloads of Klansmen were waiting. They were pulled from their car. Schwerner and Goodman were shot immediately, but Chaney, who had tried to escape, was brutally beaten before his shooting. Their car was burned and their bodies buried in an earthen dam.

Although Sheriff Lawrence Rainey saw no cause for alarm in their disappearance, claiming it was just a publicity stunt, President Johnson ordered a massive search for the missing trio. Hundreds of sailors and FBI agents combed the area, yet it took six weeks for them to recover the three bodies, and then only after an informant directed them to the dam. Seven of the killers would eventually be jailed, but the shocking incident held public attention only briefly and certainly did not result in a national crusade for black voting rights. The country was deep in the 1964 election campaign, and the Summer Project was soon forgotten.

Although the volunteers taught "freedom schools" where

they developed courses in black studies for the first time in Mississippi's history; staffed "freedom kitchens" and community centers; and plugged away at voter registration, the murders cast a pall over the Summer Project. There was real tension between whites and blacks, for, as Rita Schwerner said, "We all know that this search with hundreds of sailors is because Andrew Goodman and my husband are white. If only Chaney was involved, nothing would've been done." It had taken white deaths to command any serious government action.

Nor did the increased FBI presence have much effect on the level of violence in Mississippi. Even as the president praised the FBI's efforts there, thirty homes and churches were bombed while thirty-five civil rights workers shot at and eighty beaten. There were six related murders—and only twelve hundred new registrants to show for the expense, the tension, and the suffering. All the anguish, all the anger, welled over at James Chaney's funeral. "I've got vengeance in my heart tonight," Dave Dennis shouted. "Don't just look at me and go back and tell folks you've been to a nice service. . . . If you go back home and sit down and take what these white men in Mississippi are doing to us . . . if you take it and don't do something about it . . . then God damn your souls." That was the end of nonviolence for SNCC. From then on all its field secretaries carried weapons. Similarly, in Louisiana, first in Bogalusa and later in other towns and parishes where Klan violence was unrestrained, field workers accepted the armed protection of the militant vigilante group, Deacons for Defense and Justice.

One unambiguously positive achievement came out of Freedom Summer. Building on the previous year's "Freedom Election," COFO decided to set up a new political party in Mississippi, and through it to mount a challenge to the regular

Democratic delegation at the party's national convention in August 1964, in order to highlight the way in which blacks were excluded from the political process. The idea was Robert Moses's, and he worked tirelessly throughout the summer signing up members for the Mississippi Freedom Democratic party. By the time of its first state convention on August 6, more than sixty thousand were on the rolls. The convention elected a slate of delegates to attend the Democratic party convention in Atlantic City later in the month. There the challenge would be fought out, and Freedom Summer would dramatically intersect with national politics.

5

The National Response

PRESIDENT TRUMAN'S endorsement of virtually all the recommendations of the Committee on Civil Rights, followed by his July 1948 executive order desegregating the armed forces, placed the race issue firmly on the national agenda. Although blacks responded enthusiastically with their votes in the 1948 election, Truman's second term, dominated by the politics of anticommunism, and with the president increasingly on the defensive, was barren of accomplishment in civil rights save for the steady progress of military desegregation. Still, despite Eisenhower's landslide victory in 1952, black voters stayed with the Democrats. They expected little from the new president, who had throughout his campaign assiduously courted the white South.

Judgments on President Eisenhower's civil rights record have usually been colored by his attitude to the *Brown* decision, and rightly so. His refusal to speak out firmly in its support at any time during his presidency was a failure in leadership which cost the country dearly. Although he was fond of emphasizing the potential for moral leadership inherent in his office, Eisenhower clearly did not recognize the fight against segregation as a moral issue. "You know," he once told Earl Warren, white Southerners were only concerned "to see that their sweet little girls are not required to sit in schools alongside some big overgrown Negroes"—scarcely the view of a man who perceived either the urgency of the question or its deep moral connotations. Rather, it reflected the concerns of his party to shore up its recent gains in the Southern states. If Eisenhower is remembered for finally sending troops to Little Rock, it should also be recalled that he did nothing about Autherine Lucy, or Mansfield, Texas, or Clinton, Tennessee, incidents where the defiance of federal law was not as obvious and where the president did not feel personally betrayed, as he did by Faubus in Little Rock. Eisenhower finally appointed a black journalist, E. Frederick Morrow, to his staff, but he treated him with disdain and usually ignored his advice. Frequently Morrow found himself the butt of racist jokes by fellow staffers. He left government employment in 1960, a frustrated and bitter man, convinced the Republicans had nothing to offer on civil rights.

Nonetheless there were two civil rights bills passed during Eisenhower's second term, the first since Reconstruction. Herbert Brownell, the attorney general, understood the need for some government response to the quickening forces for change, and in 1956 he brought a four-part civil rights bill to the reluctant cabinet. Broadly the draft bill aimed at creating a civil rights commission to investigate Southern violence, to establish a civil rights division within the Department of Justice, to strengthen existing measures protecting the right to vote, and, most important, to authorize Justice Department intervention on behalf of school desegregation. Only Vice-President Nixon supported the total package; the rest of the cabinet were either skeptical or opposed. Eisenhower, disinclined to move in the area anyway, and heavily lobbied by Southern senators, quickly disavowed all aspects of the bill save those to do with voting rights.

The Civil Rights Act eventually passed in 1957. Brokered by Senate Majority Leader Lyndon Johnson, it was so weak, so lacking in enforcement possibilities that Georgia's Senator Richard Russell, an archsegregationist, could describe it as "the sweetest victory in my twenty-five years as a senator." By 1959 not a single black voter had been added to the rolls as a result of its provisions. Three years later, acknowledging the 1957 bill's failure, another act was passed, supposedly to safeguard the right to vote. It somewhat strengthened the powers of the Civil Rights Commission and the civil rights division of the Department of Justice, but it too had so much of its substance removed by the action of powerful Southerners in the Senate that Pennsylvania's Joseph Clark, one of the bill's sponsors, could describe it as "a crushing defeat." Eisenhower had once called the vote "the most effective and bloodless way" to secure equal rights for America's black citizens, and had promised to remove the barriers to it. He had manifestly failed to do so.

Neither of the two presidential candidates in 1960 had particularly strong credentials in civil rights. Of them both, Richard Nixon, who had made some forthright speeches in support of further civil rights action, was initially the most appealing. John F. Kennedy's background, as his biographer James N. Giglio has observed, "had hardly prepared him for race-related issues." He had not thought deeply about race, and if he supported civil rights legislation he did so as a matter of form rather than conviction. Furthermore his awareness that he needed the South to win election, and that his Catholicism already was a handicap there, made him particularly sensitive to Southern white attitudes. He had voted to weaken the Civil Rights Act of 1957 in several key areas, and he had criticized Eisenhower for using federal troops during the Little Rock crisis. Kennedy's choice of Lyndon Johnson as his vice-presidential running mate deepened the suspicion with which the NAACP and other civil rights bodies already viewed him.

But Nixon also had his problems. Like Kennedy, he yearned for the Southern vote, thus he avoided further declarations of support for civil rights while accepting the endorsement of various prominent segregationists. Meanwhile, the nomination secured, Kennedy made more positive noises, assuring black Americans that he fully supported his party's liberal civil rights platform and that he would move swiftly to implement it. In particular, he suggested, discrimination in federally funded housing programs would be ended by "a stroke of the pen." Then came the telephone call to Coretta King and the work behind the scenes to free her husband. Nixon decided against a similarly symbolic gesture while President Eisenhower waffled and did nothing. No doubt the spurt in black support generated by Kennedy's gesture provided his narrow margin of victory. Nixon's majority amongst whites was 52 percent; the black vote made the difference. Without it Kennedy would have lost Illinois, Michigan, New Jersey, Texas, and South Carolina—and the presidency.

Those who expected an active pursuit of civil rights goals from the new president were doomed to disappointment. The narrowness of his election victory, the strength of the conservative coalition in Congress, the need to bind the South to him in order to win legislative support, and his own and the nation's lack of a sense of urgency on the issue, decided Kennedy's agenda. Civil rights was not mentioned in his stirring inaugural address. As early as January he had told the NAACP's Roy Wilkins to expect no civil rights legislation during his first year. The deeply disturbed Wilkins doubted that simply postponing activity would result in a grateful South. Once more he feared the nation had a leader who could not see the issue's urgent moral dimension.

Not all black leaders were similarly negative toward the new administration. Kennedy was a skilled practitioner of "the politics of gesture," and for some that was sufficient in the short term. Thus he appointed Harris Wofford, an outspoken admirer of Martin Luther King, to the White House staff as adviser on civil rights. He created the President's Committee on Equal Employment Opportunity (PCEEO), ostensibly to prevent racial discrimination in businesses holding government contracts. He invited blacks to meetings and social functions in unprecedented numbers. Most important, no previous president had appointed so many blacks to government positions. In all, more than forty were selected for senior administration posts. Thurgood Marshall was only the best known of a number of black federal judges appointed during 1961. The black news magazine *Ebony* had at least some basis for its end-of-year claim that more progress toward racial equality had been made since Kennedy's inaugural "than any other year in the last decade."

The Justice Department, too, was busier under Robert Kennedy. The department instituted fifty-seven suits alleging violations of voting rights in 1961, including thirty in Mississippi. Only six such suits were instituted for the whole of the Eisenhower period, not one in the Magnolia State. More problematic was the administration's role during the Freedom Ride crisis. True, the government eventually intervened to protect the riders, not always successfully. And the mobilization of federal marshals undoubtedly prevented carnage in Montgomery. But the attorney general also made the deal with Mississippi officials that resulted in the riders ending up in the notorious Parchman Prison. Kennedy's policy of offering only limited protection to the riders may have had the support of the vast middle ground, who were not enthusiastic about the whole enterprise, but the administration's failure to appreciate the moral fervor that prompted the riders dismayed Northern liberals, white and black.

Nor did the administration's efforts on behalf of voter registration please them. When Robert Kennedy sought to encourage SNCC workers to confine their efforts to such activity, it seemed clear to his listeners that he was offering them the protection of the Justice Department if they did so. Perhaps he did, for the attorney general assumed that SNCC would concentrate its activities on the growing black urban population, where the risk of violence was not great. When instead they decided to invade the rural counties of the Mississippi Delta, the equation changed. By the end of the year SNCC workers knew they were on their own, that the FBI would not protect them even when their lives were at risk, and that the attorney general himself had placed strict limits on the scale of federal intervention. Only when it was quite clear that local authorities had no intention of upholding the law would Washington consider stepping in—far too little and far too late. As Robert Kennedy himself asserted, protection of civil rights workers was primarily a matter for local authorities. "Mississippi is going to work itself out," he said. "Maybe it's going to take a decade and maybe a lot of people are going to be killed in the meantime. . . . But in the long run I think it's for the health of the country and the stability of the system"—scarcely the voice of intense moral involvement. By the end of 1961 SNCC workers, with danger their constant companion, believed they had been betrayed by the administration, and cursed the Kennedys for it.

President Kennedy's much anticipated campaign promise, a "stroke of the pen" to end discrimination in federally financed housing programs, did not materialize in 1961 for a host of reasons. First the president thought it might jeopardize his nomination of Robert Weaver, a black, to be head of the Housing and Home Finance Agency. Then he worried what might happen to various other pieces of legislation if he went ahead with it. By the end of the year, cynical blacks began to flood the White House with cheap pens in order to help him make good his promise. He did not do so until late 1962, once the midterm congressional elections were out of the way. By this time the civil rights momentum had long since passed it by; its impact was minimal, it was now an empty gesture.

Thus at the end of its first year the Kennedy administration had displayed caution and a lack of urgency and commitment in dealing with the nation's most urgent domestic issue. Black leaders and white liberals alike were left profoundly disillusioned, convinced they could expect nothing substantial from Washington except charm, high-sounding rhetoric, and gesture.

The administration's cautious approach to civil rights continued in 1962. Indeed, the Kennedys incurred the wrath of the Civil Rights Commission, the independent watchdog body created by the Civil Rights Act of 1957. Liberal members of the commission, especially Notre Dame's Father Theodore Hesburgh, were highly critical of the administration's lack of urgency. In particular, commissioners were incensed at the lack of protection afforded the SNCC workers in Mississippi. Robert Kennedy's response, that the Justice Department was doing the best it could, was hardly encouraging.

The administration, too, was most reluctant to intervene in the Albany crisis of that year, despite city officials continuing to ignore federal court rulings. King and others expected federal action, but the Kennedys, anxious to avoid hurting the chances of a racial moderate, Carl Sanders, who was running for governor of Georgia against two extreme segregationists, declined to get involved. Besides, the policy of police chief

Laurie Pritchett meant that violence was kept to a minimum, so the crisis was never the focus of national attention. True, the president did extend moral support to the Albany demonstration, when at a press conference he admitted that he found it

> wholly inexplicable why the city council . . . will not sit down with the citizens of Albany, who may be Negroes, and attempt to secure them, in a peaceful way their rights. The United States Government is involved in sitting down at Geneva with the Soviet Union. I cannot understand why the Government of Albany . . . cannot do the same for American citizens.

For the hundreds in jail, or facing charges, that comment was not nearly enough. As Andrew Young, a King strategist, later admitted, "We thought the Kennedy administration worked against us in Albany."

Even those early Kennedy initiatives, which all had agreed seemed to promise much, were not working. In particular the PCEEO was a derisory failure. Created with great fanfare and chaired by the vice-president, with the task of preventing discrimination in the federal civil service and in firms holding government contracts, its achievements were minuscule. Over two years' work, black employment figures in the civil service advanced only about 1 percent, while among federal contractors the rise was a pathetic .01 percent. Robert Kennedy, in particular, blamed Vice-President Johnson for this result, but it was in fact a fair reflection of the New Frontier's lack of urgency or real concern in civil rights matters.

Only in the Ole Miss crisis was the administration forced to abandon its cautious approach. The duplicity and double-dealing of Governor Barnett, the arrival of out-of-state racists like General Walker, the potential, then actuality, of large-scale violence, and the continued defiance of a federal court order eventually forced decisive federal action, and order was restored in Mississippi through the intervention of federal troops. But this intervention came only after a lengthy attempt to deal with Barnett, negotiating with him by telephone over the details of Meredith's entry, treating him gently even as he continued to defy federal authority. As violence raged about them, the federal marshals sent to protect Meredith were expressly prevented from drawing their weapons unless Meredith's life was threatened. They could not protect themselves. Again, decisive action came only after a long period of temporizing, and to some, indecision.

The Ole Miss struggle did have, however, a profound effect on Kennedy's civil rights strategy. First, he knew that as a consequence the South was gone for good politically. No longer was there any use in trying to deal with the white leadership in order to retain some semblance of electoral support there. Second, it forced Kennedy to rethink his whole view of Southern history. Perhaps the traditional view of the Reconstruction period—corrupt rule by Republican conquerors and their ignorant black allies—a view to which he had subscribed, was wrong. After all, he himself was now being cast into the combined roles of Charles Sumner and Thaddeus Stevens, those ruthless despoilers of Southern rights. Certainly he dealt with his next desegregation crisis, at the University of Alabama, with greater resolve and urgency.

By that time, of course, the civil rights issue had become the major national concern. Events in Birmingham and other Southern cities in the summer of 1963 had seen to that. No longer could the president's civil rights strategy be one of caution and crisis management. He had to display national leadership, to recognize the moral nature of the struggle, and to convince the American people to do likewise. To his credit, on

June 11, 1963, in his address to the nation, John Kennedy did just that. In this most moving speech of his presidency, Kennedy kept his focus on the moral dimension of the civil rights struggle. "We are confronted primarily with a moral issue," he proclaimed.

> It is as old as the Scriptures and is as clear as the American Constitution. The heart of the question is whether all Americans are to be afforded equal rights and equal opportunities, whether we are going to treat our fellow Americans as we want to be treated. If an American, because his skin is dark, cannot eat lunch in a restaurant open to the public, if he cannot send his children to the best schools available, if he cannot vote for the public officials who represent him, if, in short, he cannot enjoy the full and free life which all of us want, then who among us would be content to have the color of his skin changed and stand in his place?

The president concluded by announcing that he would submit an all-embracing civil rights bill to Congress within a week, one which, he hoped, would remove racial discrimination once and for all from American life. That same night, Medgar Evers, Mississippi's brave NAACP secretary, was murdered in Jackson.

The bill went to Congress on June 19. It was indeed far-reaching, embodying most of the civil rights movement's priorities. Its key feature addressed discrimination in public accommodations. It guaranteed equal access to hotels, restaurants, retail establishments, libraries, theaters, swimming pools, and all places of amusement and recreation, the sites of the most violent demonstrations in preceding months. Tacitly recognizing the failure of past efforts to enfranchise Southern blacks, the bill greatly strengthened voting rights laws. Similarly, recognizing the way the *Brown* decision had been neutralized by subterfuge, intimidation, and legal delay, it empowered the attorney general to initiate school desegregation suits. It also gave the president power to withhold federal funds from state programs that discriminated, something both Roy Wilkins and Martin Luther King had been demanding for months. Although it did not give civil rights activists all they wanted—it did not address the issue of job discrimination, for example—it nevertheless represented the strongest legislative attack on racial discrimination since Reconstruction.

Kennedy went ahead with the bill in the teeth of the combined opposition of most of his staff and of his vice-president. Moreover, the Senate majority leader, Mike Mansfield warned him that the votes were not there to pass it, while its very introduction would certainly put a number of other proposals at risk, for the administration depended on the support of key Southern Democrats. "A good many programs I care about may go down the drain as a result of this," Kennedy told Martin Luther King. "We may all go down the drain." Gone was Kennedy's caution, his detached approach to the issue. Obviously this was in part due to what was happening in the streets, to the violence and disorder of the summer. But it was also due to the president's own developing moral commitment. Late in coming, it was nonetheless real. Robert Kennedy, too, had undergone a similar experience, in part the result of his meeting in May with thirteen leading black Americans, including the writers James Baldwin and Lorraine Hansberry, the entertainers Harry Belafonte and Lena Horne, and a number of SNCC and CORE activists. At first shocked by their anger and the vehemence of their criticism, he came to understand why they felt as they did. The experience of the meeting, though a searing one for him, brought home the depth of black frustration and the need for government policy to do much more to meet it. From then on Robert Kennedy pushed constantly for civil rights legislation, the only cabinet member to do so, and there can be no doubt he had a profound influence on his brother's thinking.

It was one thing to introduce a civil rights bill, quite another to secure its passage. For the rest of his life Kennedy was primarily engaged in achieving a legislative majority for the bill—no easy task, given the expressions of outrage from the Southern wing of his own party. Conservative Republicans, too, like presidential aspirant Barry Goldwater, could not countenance a bill that so augmented the intrusive power of the federal government. The president knew that to have any hope of passage, he needed to hold on to the moderates of his own party while securing Republican support from those not normally sympathetic either to him or to civil rights. Thus he was assiduous in involving Republicans in strategy sessions both before and after the bill's introduction, while attempting to prevent actions and utterances that might frighten such people away. For this reason he initially tried to dissuade King and Randolph from holding the August 28 March on Washington.

The key Republican legislators were the two minority leaders, Senator Everett B. Dirksen of Illinois and Representative Charles B. Halleck of Indiana, and the ranking Republican on the House Judiciary Committee, to which the bill was referred, Representative William M. McCulloch of Ohio. The president met frequently with Halleck and McCulloch, in particular, with whom he was able to develop a good working relationship. By the time of his assassination, the bill had cleared the House Judiciary Committee.

The Kennedys initially had more trouble keeping the House liberals in line than in winning Republican support. Civil rights activists decided that now was the time to get their whole agenda through, to press for a bill even stronger than the president's. Specifically they wanted a ban on job discrimination, enforced by a permanent Fair Employment Practices Commission, even stronger voter protection than that provided by the bill, and, most controversial of all, a provision giving the attorney general power to institute suits on behalf of private citizens against state and local governments. Such far-reaching additions were anathema to the moderate Republicans whom Kennedy was wooing but greatly appealed to the Judiciary Committee's elderly chairman, Emmanuel Celler, and other House liberals, who added them to the administration's bill. In so doing they almost wrecked it. Southern Democrats were gleeful. Their strategy was henceforth to support the strongest possible bill at all committee stages, then vote with conservative Republicans to kill it in the end.

The strategy almost worked. Only presidential intervention prevented the Judiciary Committee from rejecting the measure. Kennedy persuaded the liberals to drop their most contentious measures until only the job discrimination provisions were left. These were modified to suit the Republicans, and the bill eventually passed the committee. Still, there was much more work to be done: the Rules Committee had to be cleared, while in the Senate, Southerners, relying on the hoary tradition of never closing debate, prepared to filibuster the measure to death. There the matter rested on November 22, 1963, when John Kennedy was murdered in Dallas.

Although the civil rights leadership had been highly critical of President Kennedy for most of his term, they were devastated by his loss. They worried about the future of the civil rights bill now that he was not there to lead, and they worried especially about the commitment of the new president, Lyndon B. Johnson, to its passage. Long regarded as a man of shallow ideals, and known to be friendly with segregationist

Senate leaders like Georgia's Richard Russell, they feared the worst. Their fears were unfounded. Johnson's determination to complete Kennedy's agenda was genuine, as was his support for the civil rights bill. And his easy familiarity with the people and practices of the Senate made the possibility of passage greater rather than less.

Kennedy's martyrdom made clearing the House Rules Committee a formality. Not even its powerful chairman, the Virginia segregationist Howard Smith, could do more than carp from the sidelines. Other opponents, like Mississippi's William Colmer, were reduced to making tasteless jokes or irrelevant asides. He was worried about barbers, Colmer claimed—they were "not equipped or trained to cut the hair of the opposite race." Once the bill reached the House floor in February 1964, Smith did have one serious card to play. He insisted on adding provisions outlawing all discrimination for reasons of gender as well as race. The usual explanation for his move is that Smith hoped to kill the measure altogether. Perhaps, yet it should be noted that Smith had a long and honorable history as a supporter of equal rights for women. Whatever, his action resulted in a lively debate, and in the end he had his way, thus opening opportunities for the American women's movement that its leaders were quick to seize. The civil rights bill easily passed the House on February 10, on its way to a much harder fight in the Senate.

In the Senate the difficulty was not one of winning sufficient votes to secure passage; they may well have always been there. Rather, the problem was to get enough votes to close debate, to cut off the inevitable Southern filibuster aimed at preventing a vote on the bill. A two-thirds majority was needed, and this had never been achieved before on a civil rights measure. The president knew he could count on only forty-two Democratic votes for closure, but he needed sixty-seven. Thus twenty-five of the Senate's thirty-three Republicans would also have to support it—an impossibly tall order, it seemed. The key was the Senate majority leader, Everett Dirksen, who initially seemed decidedly lukewarm in his support. Gradually President Johnson, assisted by Robert Kennedy, wore him down, convincing him that this was a turning point in history, agreeing to a few minor amendments as the price of Dirksen's help. Southerners fought fiercely on the Senate floor, delaying passage of the bill for nearly three months. But they were defending a way of life the rest of the nation now found reprehensible. They knew the game was up when, on May 19, quoting Victor Hugo's pronouncement that no army was stronger than "an idea whose time had come," Senator Dirksen announced his support for the measure. On June 10, 1964, the Senate voted 71 to 29 to close off the Southern filibuster, the longest in American political history. Just over a week later it approved its version of the bill 73 to 27. On July 2, after the House had agreed to the Senate's amendments, President Johnson signed it into law.

As Allen Matusow has aptly written, the Civil Rights Act of 1964 "was the great liberal achievement of the decade." Those who criticized it for not going far enough missed the point. Its purpose was unambiguous: to bring legal equality to a region where none existed. This the act clearly achieved. In the weeks following its passage, segregation retreated into history as the South adjusted to the new reality with a speed that surprised everyone. Just before the act's passage, for example, a waitress had poured coffee over Andrew Young as he sought service in a St. Augustine, Florida, restaurant. Less than a fortnight later he was welcomed there with open arms. Not everyone changed overnight, of course, but as one surveys the immediate effect of the act, it is the speed of compliance, not the ferocity of resistance, that is so striking. White Southerners having lost their fight, in Leslie Dunbar's imagery, shrugged their shoulders and got on with their lives. As for black Southerners, Hartman Turnbow, an old Mississippi farmer and a stalwart supporter of the SNCC campaign, said it best: "It won't never go back where it was."

There were, of course, notable exceptions. Lester Maddox, an Atlanta restaurateur, issued his customers pickax handles for use in battering any blacks trying to enter his portals. This act of defiance got him in trouble with the law and later elected him governor of Georgia. Other restaurant owners, less volatile perhaps, promptly closed their doors, only to reopen as "private clubs." Above all there was Alabama's George Wallace. Even before the civil rights bill's passage he had declared his intention to run in a few Democratic primaries in 1964, supposedly to influence the Senate debate. In reality he hoped to expose growing white resentment of the national preoccupation with civil rights. He started campaigning in Wisconsin with neither an organization nor money, and with just about every state organization against him. He plugged away, denouncing the federal government's encroachment on basic freedoms, including the people's right to associate with whom they wished, and eventually goading Johnson's representative on the ballot, Governor John W. Reynolds, into the unwise statement that if Wallace got more than 100,000 votes the state would be disgraced. On primary day, April 7, he won 240,000 votes—34 percent of those cast. Swiftly following this by winning 30 percent in the Indiana primary and a whopping 43 percent in Maryland, he had achieved what he aimed to do—expose a raw patch in the Democratic coalition, a nerve that a clever player of racist politics could easily exploit.

Thus encouraged, Wallace announced in June 1964 his first bid for the presidency, on a third-party ticket. He was on the ballot in sixteen states by July and believed he could gain enough electoral votes to deny either candidate an electoral majority, forcing the contest into the House of Representatives. The established Southern political leadership was more realistic. By this time the Republicans had chosen as their candidate the strident Arizona conservative Senator Barry Goldwater, who had cast one of the few Republican votes against the civil rights bill. They knew Wallace, as a third-party candidate, stood no chance of defeating President Johnson, but believed Senator Goldwater might just do so. Certainly he had a chance to sweep the South. They therefore put pressure on Wallace to withdraw, and when Goldwater himself asked him to do so, he reluctantly acceded. This ended George Wallace's first bid for the presidency, but he would try again in more propitious times. Ominously, his campaign had pointed the way to the future.

Although the passage of the civil rights bill figured prominently in the litany of liberal achievements praised at the Democratic party convention in August 1964, the unfinished business of the civil rights movement cast an unexpected cloud over the proceedings. The Mississippi Freedom Democratic party, having elected sixty-eight delegates, including four whites, to the Democratic National Convention initially as a dramatic gesture of protest at the exclusion of blacks from the state's political processes, now determined to have them seated as the state's legitimate representatives. Encouraged by expressions of support from Democrats around the country, and by the fact that, unlike the Mississippi regulars, MFDP delegates were pledged to support the national platform and candidates, the MFDP representatives arrived in Atlantic City on August 24 convinced that their challenge would be successful. For four days, much to the displeasure of the president, their story was the major news of the convention.

The credentials committee heard the MFDP challenge, carried live by national television. A stream of witnesses described their harsh treatment at the hands of Mississippi authorities as they tried to exercise their basic political rights—the beatings, the jailings, the economic intimidation. It was the appearance of Fannie Lou Hamer, however, that most gripped national attention.

As she described her life, her eviction upon trying to register to vote, and, above all, the brutal beating she had received in the Winona jail, both the committee and those watching on TV were stunned. "If the Freedom Party is not seated now," she concluded, "I question America. Is this America, the land of the free and the home of the brave, where we have to sleep with our telephones off the hooks because our lives be threatened daily, because we want to live as decent human beings in America?" Telegrams flooded in supporting Mrs. Hamer and the seating of the MFDP delegates. Her moving account had captured the heart of the nation.

But not that of President Johnson. Intensely angered that the fight over seating the MFDP had already disrupted his smooth progress toward nomination, he also feared that should they win their challenge, other Southern delegates besides those of Mississippi would desert the Democratic ship. Accordingly he directed Minnesota senator and vice-presidential aspirant Hubert Humphrey to find a solution, warning him that he would lose second spot on the ticket if he failed to do so. Humphrey in turn delegated the matter to his protégé, Walter Mondale, who labored hard over the weekend. The pressure on those members of the credentials committee who had supported the MFDP was intense; much of it amounted to presidential blackmail. And Johnson was not above using the FBI to keep abreast of MFDP thinking, through wiretapping and other means of surveillance. The young would-be delegates thus received a painful introduction to the world of real politics. Eventually Humphrey and Mondale forged a compromise. Two members of the MFDP delegation would be seated, but as delegates at large, not as representatives of Mississippi. No regular Mississippi delegate would be seated unless he or she pledged allegiance to the national ticket, and no future convention would accept delegates from states that disfranchised blacks. Under extreme presidential pressure, MFDP supporters on the credentials committee accepted the compromise, and so, with reluctance, did the established civil rights leadership. Both Martin Luther King and Roy Williams, for example, recognizing that future civil rights gains could only be achieved through federal action, lobbied for the compromise, thus maintaining good relations with the president at the expense of the last vestiges of respect from SNCC.

The MFDP delegates, however, were not as politically expedient. Believing themselves, with some justice, betrayed by their friends and allies, people they had trusted, they angrily dismissed the offer as tokenism, "like the usual bone thrown to Negroes who showed signs of revolt." As usual, Mrs. Hamer put it best. They "didn't come all this way for no two votes," she said. Angrily they rejected the compromise and left the convention. Ironically the Alabama and Mississippi regular delegates did so as well.

The failure of the MFDP challenge, the way the president had manipulated the convention, and the fact that King, Bayard Rustin, and even James Farmer had in the end gone along with him, was a profound shock to SNCC activists. They believed they had been betrayed by white liberals, by the civil rights establishment, by the Democratic party, and by the federal government. As the historian Harvard Sitkoff put it, "The treatment of the Freedom Democrats snapped the frayed ties that bound SNCC to liberal values, to integration and nonviolence, and to seeking solutions through the political process." Liberals could not be trusted to follow through on their promises; blacks had to rely on themselves to gain their freedom. "Things could never be the same," wrote Cleveland Sellers. "Never again were we lulled into believing that our task was exposing injustices so that the 'good' people of America could eliminate them. We left Atlantic City with the knowledge that our movement had turned into something else. After Atlantic City, our struggle was not for civil rights, but for liberation."

With the MFDP issue out of the way, the convention proceeded as planned. Johnson was convincingly nominated and proceeded to overwhelm Goldwater in November. The Arizona senator's bleak conservatism and hard-line anticommunism enabled the president easily to straddle the political middle ground. Neither candidate paid much attention to civil rights issues in their campaigning, though Lyndon Johnson was certainly the beneficiary of federal involvement on behalf of blacks. In a landslide victory he won 61 percent of the vote, carrying forty-four states. Apart from his home state of Arizona, Goldwater won only five states, all in the Deep South—Mississippi, Louisiana, Alabama, Georgia, and South Carolina. The president carried the upper South states and with them the majority of the region's electoral votes.

The election results seemed to bear out the views of King and Rustin that black freedom could best be won through liberal politics. Ninety-four percent of the six million blacks who voted in 1964 supported the president. In the five Southern states that went for Goldwater, less than 45 percent of eligible blacks could vote, despite the reforms of the Civil Rights Act. Elsewhere in the South, black votes, often first-time black votes, gave the president his margin of victory. The Democrats also swept both houses of Congress. The way was wide open for further reforms. This, then, was the context for the last great mass campaign of the civil rights era, the drive to pass a voting rights bill in 1965.

6

The End of the Movement

FLUSHED WITH postelection euphoria, Lyndon Johnson prepared to complete the work of his political mentor, Franklin D. Roosevelt, and usher in a new era of liberal accomplishment. "Don't stay up late," he told his staffers at the inaugural ball, there was work to be done, legislation to prepare that would result in the creation of a "Great Society." Bill after bill was sent to Capitol Hill as the president gave his vision substance. But a voting rights bill was not one of them. Johnson had decided, on the advice of his staff, to submit no new civil rights legislation in 1965. He had developed new priorities, and he was still angry at the way the MFDP challenge had spoiled the Democratic convention for him. He had also developed a dislike of Martin Luther King, an enmity fanned by jealousy at *Time* magazine's choice of the civil rights leader as its 1964 Man of the Year, and chagrin that a Nobel committee had awarded King the Peace Prize. As for voting rights, surely the 1964 Civil Rights Act had taken care of that issue once and for all.

The 1964 election analysis showed otherwise. Even with the act's many provisions, only 6 percent of voting-age blacks were registered in Mississippi at year's end, 19 percent in Alabama, 32 percent in Louisiana. Goldwater had carried only those Southern states with less than 45 percent of their black population registered. Obviously there would be political benefits for the Democrats in changing this situation, yet the president believed the country had had enough of civil rights for the time being. Thus, though in his State of the Union message Johnson pledged himself to removing "every remaining obstacle to the right and the opportunity to vote," he gave no indication how he planned to do so. As had so often been the case, the man who changed the equation, who created both the situation and the opportunity for the enactment of a voting bill, was Martin Luther King. The site for what was to be his last great nonviolent direct-action campaign was Selma, Alabama.

King and his SCLC aides chose Selma only after the most careful consideration. Situated in Dallas County, in the middle of Alabama's black belt, it had both a black majority and a black voting-age population of fifteen thousand, of whom fewer than four hundred were registered to vote. As in most places with a black majority, Dallas County's whites were determined to deny blacks the vote. The Alabama chapter of the White Citizens Council had begun in Selma, and civil rights workers had long found the going extremely tough there. In 1961 the Freedom Riders had decided to bypass the town, so inflamed was white feeling against them. Most important, Dallas County had in Jim Clark a sheriff in the "Bull" Connor mold, a violent racist usually attired in a military-style uniform, complete with swagger stick, who, as Matusow wryly observed, "habitually lost his self-control at the sight of a marching Negro." King was sure that Clark would lose his control for him and provide SCLC with the television footage necessary to galvanize national action. When they arrived in the city King's staffers were delighted to see Clark wearing a huge button on his shirt with one word on it, "Never."

On January 2, 1965, King announced the voting rights campaign. "We are not asking" for the ballot, he stated, "we are demanding" it. On January 18 King and SNCC chairman John Lewis led the first march, from campaign headquarters to the county courthouse. At first Clark refrained from violence, but under pressure from Klansmen and other local racists he soon broke. The next day he punched one of the SCLC leaders, then arrested sixty-seven marchers. King and his staff were jubilant. They knew they had the sheriff where they wanted him.

Over the next weeks the demonstrators expertly tried Clark's patience as King steadily increased the tempo of the demonstrations. On February 1 he himself was arrested with 770 other marchers, many of them young schoolchildren. National attention was thus assured. Five hundred twenty more were arrested the next day, 300 the next. SCLC's strategy seemed to be working well. King himself did not remain long in jail. On February 5 he met with a group of congressmen who had come to Selma to talk about the need for a voting rights bill, and on February 9 he met with the president himself, who privately announced a change in plans. He would shortly send a voting rights message to Congress, Johnson told King. Throughout February the scale of demonstrations increased, as did the brutality of white reprisal, not only in Selma but throughout Dallas County. On February 17, in the town of Marion, a state trooper shot and killed twenty-six-year-old Jimmy Jackson as police violently broke up a voting rights demonstration.

King used the day of Jackson's funeral, March 3, to announce a dramatic escalation in the campaign. Demonstrators would leave the streets of Selma, he said, and march along the highway to Montgomery, fifty-four miles away. "I can't promise you it won't get you beaten," he told his listeners. "I can't promise you won't get scarred up a bit. But we must stand up for what is right." In Montgomery, Governor George Wallace immediately banned the march for public safety reasons, but six hundred people set out the next day, Sunday, March 7, anyway, led by King's aide Hosea Williams and John Lewis. Neither King nor Ralph Abernathy, his deputy, were there. They had both left Selma, claiming the need to minister to their congregations.

The marchers moved onto US 80, the highway to Montgomery. Scores of television cameras and print journalists recorded their progress as they reached the Edmund Pettus Bridge, just outside Selma. There they were halted by the combined forces of Jim Clark's men and a hundred state troopers commanded by Major John Cloud. With almost no warning, the marchers found themselves under vicious attack from tear gas, batons, chains, electric cattle prods, and charging horsemen. In the most savage "police riot" of the whole civil rights era, troopers and deputies attacked any who got in their way—women, children, the old, the young, the halt, the able-bodied.

Americans saw the whole event on national television and responded as King had hoped they would, with horror and anger. They telegrammed the White House, demanding presidential intervention. They petitioned their congressmen to support voting rights legislation. Four hundred Jewish, Protestant, and Catholic clergy left for Selma to show solidarity with the marchers. Tens of thousands of sympathizers marched in cities and towns throughout the nation. Jim Clark and John Cloud between them had created the national constituency for voting rights legislation.

King, in Atlanta, was shaken by the scale of the violence. He vowed to lead a second march on March 9 and asked two hundred of the nation's religious leaders to join him. But Federal District Judge Frank Johnson banned all marches, including King's, pending a federal hearing on its legality. King now found himself in the most difficult situation of his activist career. He had never before defied a federal court order. Besides, the president was putting intense pressure on him not to march, and he knew that to defy Johnson would compromise the promised voting rights legislation, the goal of the whole Selma campaign. On the other hand, clergymen were arriving by the busload expecting to march. Most ominous of all, SNCC militants who had previously held themselves aloof from the campaign were now everywhere, urging him to defy Judge Johnson's order. King announced that he would march, court order or not, but at the same time he negotiated a deal with Alabama authorities to avoid another confrontation. He would lead the marchers onto the bridge again, but this time he would stop when challenged, pray briefly, and then turn back.

The next day fifteen hundred blacks and whites followed King to the Edmund Pettus Bridge, ignorant of the charade about to be played out. Many were frightened at the prospect of another violent conflict, but they need not have worried. King halted the column when Major Cloud asked him to do so, knelt briefly in prayer, and then led his astonished supporters back to Brown Chapel in Selma. Many decided to go home there and then, but at King's entreaty some chose to stay. That night, as he walked Selma's streets with two friends, a Boston minister named James Reeb was beaten to death by white thugs.

No doubt most of the marchers were secretly relieved that March 9 had passed without violent confrontation. But the young activists of SNCC were furious. They had opposed the Selma campaign in the first place, joining it only after the violence of March 7. Now King's decision to turn back at the bridge seemed to confirm all they had come to believe of him—that he was a coward, a posturer, a man who cared more about pleasing white opinion than meeting the real needs of his people. Although they would maintain a façade of unity until the end of the Selma campaign, it was the last time they would follow his banner. The united civil rights movement, at the moment of its greatest triumph, was about to pass into history.

For triumph was what occurred in Selma, despite the turning back on the bridge. President Johnson kept his word. His aides rushed to put the finishing touches on a voting rights bill, and on March 15 the president spoke about it before a joint session of Congress and on prime-time television. It was his best speech ever. "Should we defeat every enemy," he said, "should we double our wealth and conquer the stars," if the country still denied equal rights to its black citizens "we will have failed as a people and a nation." His bill, he claimed, would establish a simple, uniform standard for voter registration which could not be used "to flout the Constitution." Federal registrars would see to that. In conclusion he spoke of the heroism blacks had displayed in their struggle against racism and second-class citizenship. "Their cause must be our cause too. It is not just Negroes, but all of us who must overcome the crippling legacy of bigotry and injustice. And we shall overcome." As the president quoted what had become the anthem of the civil rights movement, Andrew Young noticed a tear run down Martin Luther King's cheek. In Washington, Supreme Court justices joined in the standing ovation accorded the president.

Only one act remained in King's Selma campaign. Judge Johnson eventually agreed to allow the march to Montgomery, and when Governor Wallace still refused to protect the marchers, the president federalized the Alabama National

Guard and gave them the job. The marchers left, triumphantly, on March 21, and four days later King spoke to them from the steps of the state capitol. How long would it take to cleanse the nation finally of the last vestiges of racism? he asked. "Not long, because the arm of the moral universe is long but it bends toward justice." He finished by quoting the "Battle Hymn of the Republic." "How long? Not long. Because mine eyes have seen the glory of the coming of the Lord . . . his truth is marching on." In the triumph and the emotion of the moment, who could have believed that the civil rights movement would never again function with the same unity?

Johnson's voting rights bill sped through Congress, aided by swollen Democratic majorities in both houses. Its main target were the literacy tests used unfairly throughout the South to prevent blacks from registering. The bill provided that these tests could be suspended in jurisdictions where discrimination was deemed to exist (an arbitrary standard), and federal registrars could place people directly on the rolls. This and many other secondary provisions all aimed to make it impossible to deny Southern blacks the ballot. It worked, most spectacularly in the worst-offending states. By 1968 the percentage of eligible blacks registered in Alabama had increased to 53 percent, in Louisiana to 60 percent and, most dramatically of all, in Mississippi from 6 percent to 44 percent. In Selma, Alabama, where it all began, two months after the bill passed the number of black voters had already increased from 320 to 6,289. The next year Jim Clark lost office. Nothing more dramatically illustrates the importance of attaining the vote. As Allen Matusow has concluded, the 1965 Voting Rights Act "did nothing less than cleanse the poisoned atmosphere of Southern politics." King surely was right in the focus of his campaign and in his insistence that only the federal government possessed the power to effect real change.

Southern school systems nonetheless remained bitterly defended. Ten years after the *Brown* decision, less than 2 percent of the old Confederacy's black students went to school with whites. The 1964 Civil Rights Act contained the twin triggers to end this situation. One section made it possible for the attorney general to instigate school desegregation suits, thus lifting the burden from parents and community groups. But the most important weapon was Title VI. After December 31, 1964, in order to qualify for federal funds, all Southern school districts had to produce desegregation plans acceptable to the U.S. Office of Education. Title VI was, in Matusow's words, "the noose which, placed around the South's segregated schools, would be pulled tighter and tighter year by year until no life in them remained." Southern school districts, like others elsewhere, wanted and needed the federal funds flowing all over the country as a consequence of the 1965 Education Act.

At first Southerners hoped that the worst provisions of Title VI could be evaded by intelligent tokenism, but they were wrong. Office of Education officials, as they became more familiar with the desegregation process, constantly revised their desegregation guidelines, tightening up compliance procedures, blocking loopholes, and setting progress requirements that had to be met. The pressure on the Office of Education from Southern legislators was intense, but its officers stuck to their guns. The percentage of blacks attending school with whites in the South rose 10 percent between 1966 and 1967, and would keep on rising as the federal courts, at the end of 1966, finally came to the aid of the education bureaucracy. Then the Fifth Circuit Court of Appeals upheld the legality of Office of Education desegregation procedures, ordering "Officials administering public schools . . . to bring about an integrated unitary system in which there are no Negro schools and no white schools—just schools."

This judgment spelled the end of school segregation in the South. The federal courts had legitimated bureaucratic action, now they would work with the bureaucracy to enforce the law. Offending school districts could either desegregate and receive federal aid or defy Office of Education guidelines, lose their aid—and then be forced by the courts to desegregate anyway. Even the most unreconstructed Southern politicians and public officials now knew the game was up. In May 1968 the Supreme Court finally clarified its position on the pace of desegregation, rejecting a voluntary desegregation plan from New Kent County, Virginia, because it smacked of tokenism and failed, in the Court's view, to end discrimination "root and branch." That September, when the school year began, the number of black students in desegregated Southern schools had risen to 32 percent. By 1972 the percentage was 46; outside the South it was only 28. The Southern caste structure, as it had manifested itself in separate school systems, was finally a thing of the past, almost twenty years after the Supreme Court had declared it to be so.

By this time, 1972, the civil rights movement had long since fallen into disarray. For the young activists of SNCC, the failure of the MFDP challenge in 1964 was the ultimate betrayal. Never again would they work with white liberals or place their trust in the political process. The SCLC leadership that had urged them to accept the compromise were also betrayers. King's behind-the-scenes negotiations over the Selma march completed the process of alienation. Although the SNCC members marched with him to Montgomery, they did so only because it suited their own purposes. Never again would they work with the man they now derisively referred to as "De

Lawd," or even take what he said seriously. By 1965 years of living and working in the battle zone of the rural South had taken its toll on the young men and women of SNCC. They had lost their commitment to integration, had been betrayed both by white liberals and the civil rights establishment, and now carried guns, symbolic of their rejection of nonviolence. The black psychiatrist Alvin Poussaint, who worked with them, reported that from 1965 he "frequently had to calm Negro civil rights workers with large doses of tranquilizers for what I can describe clinically only as acute attacks of rage."

Often their rage was directed at each other, as the organization became increasingly beset with factional conflict over future programs. James Forman wanted to reorganize SNCC into a highly disciplined corps, placing much more emphasis on political activism than community organization. Robert Moses, and those like him who had been with the organization from the beginning, resisted this projected shift. In a bitter struggle, Forman and his supporters won control of the agency, leaving Moses's faction powerless on the periphery. Most of its members soon left SNCC. Moses himself quit not only the organization but the country, departing for Africa.

Yet the interracial struggles were less ferocious than those between the organization's black and white members. Since 1963 whites had worked in Mississippi in significant numbers. The high point was Freedom Summer in 1964, but even in 1965 three hundred white students arrived for the summer projects. From the start there was racial tension, often enough to affect seriously the work project. The flash point, more often than not, was sex. White women were the catalyst. For many black men, these women symbolized the heretofore unattainable, objects both of desire and danger during the segregation era. To have a relationship with a white girl therefore involved a complex set of emotional responses, yet many black men were attracted. White women, too, were quick to reciprocate, often out of feelings of guilt. Then they encountered the jealousy of the black women whose men they had taken. Sexual tension of this nature nearly wrecked the SNCC summer program in 1965. It reinforced the growing conviction of the new leadership that working with whites was a thing of the past, that the integrationist ideal was hopelessly misplaced.

No one expressed this antiwhite, black separatist tendency within SNCC more fiercely than the man who in 1966 became its president. A native of Trinidad who had grown up in New York City, and a scarred veteran of the civil rights battles, Stokely Carmichael had long since given up any notion of the essential goodness of most white people and the moral superiority of nonviolence. As early as 1964 he had bitterly opposed using whites in the Freedom Summer project. On becoming president of SNCC, he moved swiftly to cut the organization's remaining ties with white support, even if this meant summarily dismissing its few white staffers—men like Bob Zellner, who had been with SNCC from the beginning and who had also been beaten and jailed and spent the last five years living in daily fear of their lives. There could be no place for Zellner in Carmichael's SNCC with its notions of black separatism and its new and ominous-sounding slogan, "Black power."

After the failure of the MFDP challenge, Carmichael had been single-minded in his insistence that blacks needed their own political structures. In 1965 he had founded in Lowndes County, Alabama, a local all-black political party, which took as its symbol the black panther, the precursor of the later Oakland, California–based organization. The SNCC presidency gave Carmichael the ideal position through which to act on his nationalist convictions.

White America first heard the slogan "black power" in June 1966. James Meredith, as usual acting alone, had embarked on a walk from Memphis to Jackson to show his black fellow citizens that it was now possible to travel on the state's highways without fear. He had scarcely left Memphis before he was shot and unable to continue. Civil rights activists rushed to complete the walk. Martin Luther King spoke of the continuing need for nonviolence as he walked the highway, but it was Stokely Carmichael who seized national attention. He told those whites who had joined the march to go home. Then, addressing a cheering crowd in Greenwood, Mississippi, he had given the integrationist ideal its death knell. "We want black power," he shouted. King expressed his profound disapproval, but it did not matter. The cry for "black power" would soon be the battle slogan of Carmichael's SNCC.

By 1966 the demand for "black power," though relatively new to the South, had become a familiar one in the nation's black ghettos. Although Malcolm X had been murdered in Harlem early in 1965, many came forward to claim his separatist mantle. He was a model for every aspiring nationalist, including Carmichael, while many echoed his message of hatred toward whites. "Black power" unsettled an America that in the mid-1960s was further shocked and frightened by the riots in its ghettos. Beginning in Watts, a black section of Los Angeles, in 1965 and culminating in the worst riot in a century, the 1967 burning of black Detroit, scores of American cities experienced similar disorder, though on a smaller scale, during the period. Their causes were many, but as expressions of black rage and black despair they were both frightening and frustrating. They seemed to make a mockery both of the notions of progress which still drove Martin Luther King, and the idea that in cleansing the South of segregation, the nation's racial problems had been solved. For Carmichael and his SNCC colleagues, however, the riots affirmed their belief that violent revolution was imminent, that their "black power" message was being translated into violent action in the ghetto streets.

King reacted to these developments first with bewilderment, then with growing dismay. As he listened to the hate-filled rhetoric of the black nationalists and watched the flames rise in American cities, he was forced to recognize how little ten years of civil rights agitation and his message of nonviolence had touched American ghettos outside the South. He had been a regional leader combating a regional evil, legally enforced segregation. But the blighted lives of ghetto blacks were not a consequence of racism enshrined in law but the pervasive effect of centuries of discrimination and lack of opportunity. Nothing brought this home to King more profoundly than his visit to the still smoldering Watts ghetto of Los Angeles in 1965. Although there had been riots in New York, Rochester, and Philadelphia the preceding year, it was the violence in Watts, with forty-five square miles ravaged, thirty-four deaths, and more than four thousand arrests, that underscored the tinderbox nature of America's slums. King arrived in Watts ready to talk once more about his dream but found his audience mocking and irreverent. "Hell, we don't need no damn dreams," was one response, "we want jobs." When he invited people to join hands and sing "We Shall Overcome," they replied instead, "Burn, baby, burn." Watts was not Montgomery. There was no community there, no shared religious culture, not even a defined and oppressive power structure to attack. King had nothing to say to lower-class urban blacks. He left after a few days, deeply depressed.

In the following weeks his dejection led him to the conviction that the civil rights movement had to move north, that the next step must be an attack on the urban poverty and social blight that had created places like Watts. Surely the strategies that had worked so well in the South could be successfully applied to new sets of problems. Surely blacks in other parts of the nation could use nonviolent direct action to further their own ends, as a means both of diffusing their anger and of pressuring local power structures. Surely it would be seen as preferable to rioting or to "black power" separatism as a means of attacking ghetto poverty and neglect. Thus King decided to move his mission north, to the slums of Chicago.

King and the SCLC went to Chicago at the beginning of 1966 to launch the "Campaign to End Slums." He was ebullient on arrival, confident that he would have the support of the city's white liberals, who had enthusiastically backed his work in the South, and of President Johnson, who had only recently announced his own War on Poverty. Although he knew Chicago's Mayor Richard J. Daley did not exactly welcome his arrival, he believed that, faced with a disciplined mass movement, Daley would be forced to negotiate, just as Southern mayors had done. "We are going to create a new city," exulted James Bevel, King's Chicago lieutenant. "Nobody will stop us."

Nine months later King and his staff knew just how misplaced their optimism had been. First, blacks, as in Watts, failed to respond as they had in the South. They well knew what "freedom" was in King's terms. They were not segregated, they had the right to vote—usually for Mayor Daley—and they knew how little it meant to their daily lives. Thus, though they came to listen to King, they did not stay to march. James Bevel had predicted he could easily produce 100,000 marchers; he never turned out even half that number. And despite his emphasis on nonviolence, Chicago blacks rioted during King's stay in the city, and there was nothing he could do to prevent it. The people were no longer his.

Second, Mayor Daley was not "Bull" Connor or Jim Clark. The mayor, alert to the demands of many groups, including real estate interests, had little intention of negotiating seriously with King, though he was equally determined that the civil rights leader be treated with respect. Thus he welcomed King to his city, gave strict orders to the police against using force or intimidation, and emphasized his own commitment to civil rights and equality of opportunity. King, who depended on the brutality of his opponents in order to arouse national anger, was kept off guard by Daley's tactics. Lacking billy clubs and fire hoses, it was hard to create drama for television.

Not until July did King seize on a tactic that brought the television cameras to Chicago. Because marching in their own space was getting them nowhere, blacks would henceforth march in Chicago's white neighborhoods to protest their own restriction to the ghettos. The working-class whites—Italians, Poles, and Irish—who lived in the areas King had selected did not appreciate these invasions. They shouted racist insults, threw rocks (on August 5 King himself was injured by a missile), and demonstrated convincingly that racial tension was alive and well in the city. Only the valiant work of Chicago's police prevented marchers from being overrun on several occasions. Mayor Daley was furious. He knew that his protection of the marchers was eating into his white working-class support.

King's tactics, however, fatally weakened his position among white liberals, who were increasingly bothered about the disorder he was creating, with its potential for widespread rioting. When he announced plans to march through the notoriously racist suburb of Cicero, most of them deserted the cause. Chicago's Cardinal John P. Cody, formerly a strong supporter, asked him to end the protests. Others, less restrained, denounced him as an outside agitator who, by his excesses, had set back by many years progress toward integrated neighborhoods in Chicago. Chicago's liberals may have supported direct action when it was confined to the South. They were less happy about it on their doorstep.

Increasingly isolated, King desperately sought a way out. Daley, anxious to reduce the tension, was happy to oblige. On August 26, civil rights leaders and city officials signed an agreement that committed the city, the real estate industry, the public housing authority, every relevant body, in fact, to uphold fair-housing principles and promote black resettlement throughout the urban area. Hailing it as a great victory, King called off his demonstrators and prepared to leave Chicago. He promised to return if there was no progress toward the agreement's implementation.

Predictably there was none. King left, the ghetto settled down, and Daley and the other signatories conveniently forgot the agreement. As he promised, King returned the next year, not to lead further demonstrations for open housing but to mount a voter registration drive, hoping to shake the black vote loose from Daley's grip. It was, like the whole Chicago enterprise, a failure. Daley easily won reelection in April 1967 for a fourth term as mayor. Despite King's efforts, blacks voted for him 4 to 1. Fair housing, like everything else, could not be dealt with effectively at the local level but would require federal action to be achieved. President Johnson had proposed such legislation in 1966, but Congress, increasingly preoccupied with the escalating war in Vietnam, showed as little disposition to enact it as Johnson did to press for it. As Martin Luther King retreated empty-handed from Chicago, many blamed him for setting back, rather than created pressure for, the cause of fair housing. It was a far cry from Birmingham.

The failure of the Chicago movement not only left King increasingly isolated within the shattered civil rights structure, it fueled his changing attitude toward American society's most basic assumptions. The nation's growing involvement in the Vietnam War had started him on this course. Although he had been troubled since 1965 by the thrust of American policy in Vietnam, he had been reluctant to speak publicly about these doubts, dependent as he was on presidential support for his domestic program. By 1967, however, he could no longer remain silent. The war was taking billions of dollars away from the struggle against poverty; it was sending young men, disproportionately black, to their deaths in Southeast Asia; most important of all, it reinforced the use of violence as an instrument of national policy. How could he, King asked, continue to preach nonviolence at home while the government exalted its use abroad? King now became one of the war's most trenchant opponents, and with this came a profound disillusion with the moral underpinning of his own society. America, he claimed in 1967, had become "the greatest purveyor of violence in the world." The Vietnam War had made this obvious, but the root causes lay in the country's deep economic and social inequalities, in the pervasive class-based exploitation of the poor, and in its embedded racism.

What had happened in Chicago, in King's mind, exemplified this deeper malaise. He had always thought of racism as primarily a Southern problem. He knew that racial discrimination persisted in other regions of the country, but he had believed it was a secondary concern. Chicago had ended all that. The mobs there had shaken him to the core. He had never before seen such hostility, such hate, not even in Birmingham. His faith in American democracy itself, he said, had been profoundly altered by the experience. The civil rights movement had not defeated "the monster of racism," he told his staff. "We have got to see that racism is still alive in our country. And we have got to see that the roots of racism are very deep." Racism, he had learned, was not simply irrational prejudice but was embedded deep in the country's economic and social system. His battle in Chicago had taught him that. His Southern victories may have been profound, but they had done nothing for the teeming masses in the North's ghettos. Only a radical change in the nation's economic structure could help them, could eliminate the economic disparity between black and white, between the "haves" and the "have nots." This would require political action far beyond the agenda of American liberalism—a move toward a kind of socialism which most of the nation would find alien and hostile. Yet it was toward this goal that King's energies were henceforth directed.

In the last year of his life King made the crusade against poverty his exclusive concern. In the fall of 1967, after another series of devastating urban riots, he announced plans for a "Poor People's Campaign" the following spring. As with his Chicago venture, his aim was to provide a constructive alternative to violence, one that would also change the nation's priorities. He hoped to lead thousands of the nation's dispossessed, of all races, to Washington. There they would stay. Living in "tent cities," they would lobby legislators, march for action, and keep the country focused on the plight of the underprivileged. They would not, however, resort to violence, nor would they be advocates of "black power." Like every movement he had led since those far-off Montgomery days, King's Poor People's Campaign would be both nonviolent and integrated.

King quickly convinced himself that the campaign could

save America. Certainly it was bold in its conception. In its inclusiveness it challenged those who were now his opponents, the "black power" ideologues of the increasingly separatist SNCC, while its expressly class-based structure struck at the foundations of American capitalism. Many within SCLC doubted that he could pull it off, or even that it was worth the attempt. James Bevel, for example, believed that SCLC should instead commit its resources to the growing antiwar movement. But King threw himself into the organization of the Poor People's Campaign with an optimism he had not shown for many months. He was greatly heartened in early March 1968 when Robert Kennedy belatedly decided to challenge President Johnson for the Democratic presidential nomination. King not only believed that Kennedy would win, he had become convinced that the two men shared the same dream for the future, that Kennedy too had come to see the centrality of the issue of systemic economic inequality.

In mid-March, King took time out from the final planning of the Poor People's Campaign in order to help the mostly black striking garbage workers of Memphis, Tennessee, who were locked in bitter conflict with the city administration over wages and union recognition. He addressed a major rally in Memphis on March 18, which went so well that he promised to return ten days later to lead a march to city hall, just like the old days. But the march turned sour, with violence and rioting—not provoked by the city's police this time, but by the deliberately provocative actions of young black gang members, whom neither King nor the march organizers could control. It took the intervention of the National Guard to restore order, leaving King, the symbol of nonviolence, so deeply depressed that he even contemplated calling off the whole Poor People's Campaign.

King quickly recovered his élan, however, cheered by the

news that President Johnson had decided not to run for re-election. On April 3 he returned to Memphis and that evening spoke off the cuff to a mass meeting. Returning first to the themes of his first speeches, in the Montgomery years, he then spoke of his own future. "Like anybody," he concluded,

> I would like to live a long life. Longevity has its place. But I'm not concerned about that now. I just want to do God's will. And He's allowed me to go up to the mountaintop, and I've looked over. And I've seen the promised land. I may not get there with you. But I want you to know tonight that we as a people will get to the promised land. So I'm happy tonight. I'm not worried about anything. I'm not fearing any man. "Mine eyes have seen the glory of the coming of the Lord."

It was one of the most powerful speeches of his public career—and the most prophetic. The following afternoon, upbeat and confident, Martin Luther King was murdered as he joked with his aides on the balcony of the Lorraine Motel. His assassin was James Earl Ray, a hired killer. Who paid Ray remains a mystery to this day.

King's death occasioned a national outpouring of grief, a fresh wave of rioting, and, among his racist opponents, private rejoicing. The president ordered flags to be flown at half-staff and proclaimed a national day of mourning. Yet many African Americans questioned the depth of white angst. No one doubted Robert Kennedy's sincerity, however, when, less than an hour after the assassination, he told an angry mob in Indianapolis's black ghetto that King had "dedicated his life to love and to justice," and had died because of this. They owed it to his memory, he said, not to transfer the anger they understandably felt into hatred for "all white people," nor to give way to violence. "Rather let us dedicate ourselves," he concluded, "to what the Greeks wrote so many years ago: to tame the savageness of man and to make gentle the life of this world. Let us dedicate ourselves to that, and say a prayer for our country and for our people."

Historians have since claimed that Kennedy's presence there was the main reason the Indianapolis ghetto did not erupt into flames that night. Many others did. Violence, looting, and death visited 125 cities as rioters fought police and troops, "liberating" their districts, in the words of "black power" advocates. It was only temporary, if "liberation" it ever was. By April 11 the "revolt" was over, put down by federal troops. Forty-six people were dead, 35,000 injured, and more than 20,000 arrested.

On April 10 Congress passed the 1968 Civil Rights Act, the last of the era, which had long been stalled in the Senate. Probably the shock of King's death had pried it loose. Concerned chiefly with fair housing, it outlawed discrimination in the sale and rental of housing, strengthened the hand of the Justice Department to initiate housing discrimination suits, took aim at other discriminatory housing practices, and made it a federal crime to kill, injure, or intimidate people exercising their civil rights or encouraging others to do so. True, its provisions were difficult to enforce, but it may have aided the slow trend toward open housing that first appeared in the 1970 census. It was also the last legislative victory of the decade for the civil rights lobby and its liberal allies.

The Poor People's Campaign continued, but without King the planned march degenerated into an ill-organized, unfocused ramble as his successors jockeyed for power and position. Few even noticed when, in the demoralizing wake of Robert Kennedy's assassination, and after equally demoralizing rains, "Resurrection City," the tent community the marchers had established on the Mall in Washington, was quietly packed away. The campaign had been a dismal failure, Congress was unmoved, and the country, traumatized by assassination and by the divisiveness of the Vietnam War, and increasingly occupied by the forthcoming presidential election, was downright hostile. As for the civil rights movement itself, King's death had dramatized what was already obvious. It was over. Its former contributing agencies and allies lay shattered—demoralized, disunited, and often mutually antagonistic. They spoke different languages now, and pursued different goals. The greatest social movement in twentieth-century American history, it had transformed the American South but deserved a nobler end.

7

The New South

ALTHOUGH IT IS still possible today to replicate Wilson Head's bus journey of 1946, few would bother to do so. In the New South of expressways and frequent-flyer specials, most travelers would prefer swifter means. Whatever the choice, no one would experience what the young veteran did then. Discrimination in public transportation and in travel facilities has long been a thing of the past, one of the first and most obvious symbols of the transformed South. How much has changed since 1968 because of the civil rights movement? How much remains the same?

In 1976 an oddly assorted group sang in triumph at the conclusion of the Democratic National Convention. With the party's newly selected candidate for president, former Georgia governor Jimmy Carter, there was Martin Luther King's widow, Coretta Scott King, and Alabama's Governor George Wallace, now crippled by a would-be assassin's bullet. Together they led the delegates in a rousing chorus of the civil rights anthem "We Shall Overcome." In so doing they symbolized starkly the transformation of national politics the movement had engendered. Carter, governor of a Southern state, could not possibly have aspired to national office before the events of the 1960s. To achieve power in Georgia he would had to have made the traditional segregationist noises and thus rendered himself politically unacceptable at a higher level. Wallace, the archsegregationist of the 1960s, was still in power, kept there largely by the new black voters of Alabama. After he had candidly confessed his past sins and begged their forgiveness, they recognized they had more in common with him and his progressive impulses than with the conservatism and neoracism of the resurgent state Republicans. Mrs. King was keeper of the memory, the connection with the man who, more than anyone else, brought it about. Since the 1960s only two Democrats, both ex-governors, have reached the White House. Both were from the South, and both depended on black votes to provide them with victory. Neither could possibly have been considered for the presidency before Southern blacks were able to take part in the region's politics.

When Andrew Young and Barbara Jordan were elected to the U.S. House of Representatives in 1972, they were the first of a growing number of African Americans sent to Washington from the old Confederacy. All states now have at least one black representative, and most have more, including Alabama and Mississippi. Solidly Democratic, they include veteran civil rights activists like John Lewis as well as young men and women who have grown up in the post–civil rights South. Beneficiaries of the reforms of the 1960s, they are vitally concerned to prevent any loss of commitment and have worked well with black representatives from other regions to form the powerful congressional Black Caucus. Some of them have also benefited from creative redistricting plans which have resulted in Southern congressional districts with solidly black majorities but with little geographic or social contiguity, most notably in North Carolina and Georgia. These the Supreme Court has recently called into question, and the number of black representatives may decline as a result. No African American has been elected to the Senate since Edward Brooke represented Massachusetts there in the late 1960s and 1970s, though in 1990 Charlotte's popular former mayor, Harvey Gantt, came closer to unseating North Carolina's archconservative Senator Jesse Helms than any of his white challengers. Ironically, one of Helms's key campaign aides that year was James Meredith.

It is at the state and local levels, however, that the impact of the Voting Rights Act is most obvious—in the numbers of Southern blacks now registered to vote, in those holding office, and in the effect of black political involvement on white politicians. By the mid-1980s black voter registration had reached the same basic level as white, around 66 percent, with Mississippi leading the way. More than three-quarters of its eligible black citizens were registered by 1984, dramatic testimony of the act's effectiveness, recalling the 1964 figure of 6 percent. Throughout the South, blacks took their places in state legislatures, overwhelmingly as Democrats, and in far greater proportion than in the nation as a whole, though nowhere near their population ratio. Their number was greater in Alabama and Mississippi, but by the 1990s all Southern state legislatures had substantial black blocs. Some, such as the former speaker of the North Carolina house, Dan Blue, achieved substantial statewide influence; others, like Jesse Oliver from Dallas, who steered a far-reaching health-care measure through the Texas legislature in 1986, became effective legislative advocates of particular measures or concerns, able to build coalitions of interest with white politicians. One of these, Douglas Wilder of Virginia, played the post-racial political game so effectively that he was elected the state's lieutenant governor in 1985 and then, four years later, the only African American ever to become a state governor. Commentators at the time were quick to call him the most potent symbol of the South's changed political atmosphere.

Black political participation has transformed Southern local politics. It was not long before the region's major cities, Atlanta, Richmond, Raleigh, even Birmingham and Jackson, had each elected black mayors, men who achieved power, like their Northern counterparts, by combining black votes with those of liberal whites. Once in power they transformed local administration, eventually achieving the cooperation of the predominantly white business leadership. Men like Maynard Jackson in Atlanta, Henry Marsh and Roy West in Richmond, Harvey Gantt, and Birmingham's Richard Arrington all built successful biracial coalitions of local elites which enabled them to retain power while removing the last traces of segregation from city administrations.

As the region's cities went, so did its small towns and hamlets. Here the brutal face of segregation was often at its most naked, and here the franchise transformed everything. Throughout the South the most obviously repressive symbols of the old regimes—the mayors, the sheriffs, the police chiefs—lost office, in many cases to African Americans where they were of sufficient number on the electoral rolls. If not they were replaced by whites who, recognizing the realities of the changed situation, spoke and acted accordingly. The picture of Sparta, Mississippi, in the long-running television series "In the Heat of the Night" may be overdrawn and sentimentalized, but it does contain an important kernel of truth. The Southern demagogue, the overtly racist politician, is a thing of the past. He was swept away in the post-1965 tide—unless he atoned for his past sins and promised to do better.

No one reinvented himself more completely than segregation's former apotheosis, George Wallace. On the twentieth anniversary of the Montgomery Bus Boycott, Martin Luther King's archenemy spoke in the Dexter Avenue Baptist Church, King's old church. He told of his conversion and his suffering. As he was wheeled away, the black congregation reached out to him in empathy. They gave him their votes as well, keeping him in power. Perhaps, too, they believed him when he said he had sinned. Certainly, as David Goldfield tells us, Robert Strickland did. He had marched with Martin Luther King along Highway 80 in 1965, singing, "Ain't gonna let George Wallace turn us around," but in 1982, during the Democratic gubernational primary, he was with Wallace all the way. Wallace was like Saul, he said. He had been "struck down and then got up to do good. . . . He's said he regretted the past, and down here the folks believe him. That's all." When Wallace was sworn in the next year for his last term as governor, an African American recited the pledge of allegiance, a black judge administered the oath, and a black minister led the benediction.

Such symbols abound throughout the region, even in Mississippi. When Fanny Lou Hamer died in 1977, the state legislature stood with heads bowed before passing a resolution of appreciation for her service to the state. Seven years later, when the 1965 Voting Rights Act came up for renewal, Senator Stennis was an enthusiastic supporter, as was the old 1948 Dixiecrat, South Carolina's Strom Thurmond. Symbols of another kind were Arkansas's former governor Orval Faubus, who ended his working life as a bank teller in his hometown, and Deputy Sheriff Cecil Price of Philadelphia, Mississippi. Price eventually went to jail for depriving Schwerner, Goodman, and Chaney of their civil rights in 1964. Twenty-five years later he too was back in his hometown, working as a gardener for the city, which by this time had a black mayor.

While it is important to recognize these symbols of profound change, it should not be thought that Southern politics has been cleansed of racism. The rise of the Republican party in the region, and the appeal within it of men like Jesse Helms and Lauch Fairclough of North Carolina, of Newt Gingrich, of Oliver North, even of David Duke, give the lie to that. Republicans in the South and in the nation do not speak in racial terms but often use code words and phrases when attacking such policies as affirmative action or supporting law-and-order campaigns. They genuinely represent a conservative tide in the United States which has flowed strongly throughout the past two decades, with roots spread far wider than the civil rights legislation. The two-party South is a creature of the civil rights years, with the region's Republican party overwhelmingly white and affluent, and its black vote largely Democratic. Blacks participate in Southern politics at all levels now, but in an increasingly racially divided two-party system.

The practice of combining the bulk of the black vote with a minority of white votes to elect moderate Democrats to state and federal office worked well for Jimmy Carter in Georgia, Dale Bumpers in Arkansas, Reuben Askew in Florida, and even William Waller in Mississippi, in the 1970s. It continued in the 1980s with Arkansas's Bill Clinton, Alabama's Howell Heflin, and North Carolina's Terry Sanford and Jim Hunt. Now, given the recent conservative tide, it seems to have lost its force. The defeat of Tennessee's Senator James Sasser in 1994 is a potent example of this. Republicans, appealing to an exclusively white electoral bloc, have recently achieved substantial success, and look set to continue to do so. Nevertheless, in terms of its aims to enable blacks to participate equally with whites at all levels of politics, the voting provisions of the civil rights movement triumphantly succeeded.

What of the ending of the dual education system? Here the

record has been mixed. Although legal segregation is a thing of the past, thoroughly integrated school systems have not necessarily developed. The *Brown* decision has had its most obvious effect at the college and university level. At Ole Miss and at the University of Alabama, football still rules, and black athletes now dominate the squads. In the basketball-mad Carolina Piedmont, Michael Jordan is only the best known of a string of outstanding black basketball players who have kept the University of North Carolina and Duke University at the cutting edge of the sport for more than two decades. But sport is just the most obvious symbol of the integration of Southern higher education. Universities and colleges compete for the best black faculty and the most promising undergraduate students. So do graduate and professional schools throughout the region. Ironically the integration of higher education has taken place at the expense of the pre–civil rights black colleges and universities, those that once provided the shock troops for the movement. Now part of integrated systems, yet often unable to make up for decades of scarce resources, their best faculty constantly under threat from better-paying, previously all-white institutions, and increasingly unlikely to attract top students, they have had a hard time of it recently. A few, like North Carolina Central University (previously North Carolina College for Negroes), have stayed in the mainstream by attracting white students to its professional schools, but most are perched precariously on the academic margin. Many of the region's private black colleges have closed their doors, their purpose done.

At the high school and elementary school levels, the Supreme Court by 1970 had struck down the last attempts to maintain tokenism in Southern school districts, insisting on immediate desegregation. The following year it upheld the Charlotte-Mecklenburg school district's controversial plan to achieve racial balance in the system by extensive busing, thus heralding a new phase in the school desegregation story. All over the nation, children were transferred out of their neighborhoods to schools in other parts of the city. Busing was the most effective means of achieving racial balance, yet it produced bitter white resentment, mostly racially motivated but compounded by the seeming destruction of the notion of the neighborhood school. The most violent resistance to busing occurred not in the South but in the Irish suburbs of South Boston.

Within the South, most white parents reluctantly went along with busing and "instant integration." A significant number, however, chose to abandon the public school system altogether. Private schools flourished in the South in the 1970s. Some were well planned and well financed, catering to the children of the professional elite and sufficiently inclusive to enroll those black applicants whose parents could afford the fees. Most, however, were "segregation academies," poorly resourced and staffed, often with connections to the renascent religious right, and with a totally white student body. Many were fly-by-night affairs. Unable to qualify for state or federal funding, they would not survive once the worst of the integration crisis was past.

Often these schools themselves fell victim to the most effective means of slowing the pace of school integration: white flight to the suburbs, out of the city school district and into the county. In most of the South's larger cities, residential segregation had effectively been achieved by the mid-1980s, and school district boundaries reflected this. The increasing concentration of blacks in the cities' centers, where housing was cheaper, and where most public housing projects were located, complemented white movement to the suburbs. In Durham, North Carolina, the city schools, which had been 55 percent black in 1970, were more than 87 percent black in 1990; those in the county were 70 percent white. In this situation, busing could only be effective if separate school systems agreed to merge, as in Charlotte-Mecklenburg, but most have been reluctant to do so. Thus dual school systems have effectively been reestablished in the South's larger cities, and this the courts can do little to prevent.

But the most racially balanced school systems in the nation are also in the South, especially in its small towns. There immediate integration usually meant combination, the closing of schools, and the merging of students and faculty as the dual system collapsed. True, in such towns the worst of the segregation academies briefly flourished. And when these towns have become, to some degree, suburbs of larger professional communities, as in the old textile town of Burlington, North Carolina, quality private schools often serve the elites of both races. Yet in these towns blacks and whites go to school together in greater numbers than anywhere else in the nation. There white parents formerly most resistant to desegregation now say they favor integrated schools provided "quality education" is maintained. In such towns the importance of the neighborhood school reflects a value judgment that both black and white parents hold dear. Even in suburban schoolrooms, the situation in 1996 is nothing like that of 1956. There are always some black students and, equally important, black faculty, even black principals. The reestablishment of de facto dual educational systems is partial and does not reflect a resegregation of public life.

The dispensation of Southern justice, too, has been profoundly changed as a result of the civil rights revolution and subsequent Supreme Court action. If African Americans now participate in the making of Southern laws, they also participate in their application. Black judges sit on state supreme courts and on various appellate courts, right down to the local level. Black and white prosecutors, black and white defense attorneys permeate the jurisdictions. Black and white men and women routinely serve on juries, for it can no longer be otherwise. The business of justice, then, is no longer a white nor a male preserve. Southern juries can no longer protect their own, as they did the murderers of Emmet Till, for example, nor can they engage in legal lynching. Again, it would be myopic to pretend that race is never a factor in criminal proceedings, or that the law in the South is invariably even-handed in its application. Certainly the inmates of Southern prisons remain disproportionately black—and disproportionately poor—as do prisoners throughout the nation. Yet Southern law is manifestly no longer the white man's law, to be applied to black Southerners by whim or by notions of social control. It now reflects the constitutional guarantees of equal protection. The importance of this change on the conditions of Southern black life can scarcely be overestimated.

What of the ultimate means of social control, white violence? The burning of three black churches in rural Alabama late in 1995 indicated that there are still relics of the pre-1964 years around. In the 1970s membership in the Ku Klux Klan tripled as whites violently reacted to the pace of social change. Lynchings occurred in Alabama and North Carolina in 1979, and at least twelve in Mississippi in 1980, while the next year, in Georgia, a black woman was brutally killed. The Klan was suspected of being behind all of them. Nevertheless in the 1980s the law caught up with the Order. In Mobile, Alabama, a group of Klansmen who had murdered nineteen-year-old Michael Donald in 1981 in order to demonstrate the continuing strength of the secret society, were sent to jail for life on the recommendation of a predominantly white jury. Later, after a civil suit in which she was awarded damages of

$10 million, the Alabama Klan's assets were turned over to Donald's mother. In 1984 in North Carolina, an all-white Iredell County jury convicted six Klansmen of the systematic violation of the civil rights of local residents. They too went to jail. In Wake County, North Carolina, in 1993, again after a civil suit, the local Klan's assets, including its hall, were turned over to the local branch of the NAACP. The Klan still exists but on the fringes of Southern life, its propensity for violence much diminished by legal attack, by shifting community mores, and by the changed consciousness of black Southerners.

Of all the requirements of the 1964 Civil Rights Act, the public accommodations provision was most rapidly and generally complied with. Even in the most rural counties of the South, little remains of the old divisions, while in the cities and towns blacks and whites eat and drink together, watch movies together, and mingle freely in diners and restaurants, bars, motels, hotels, and theaters. Generally they do not worship together—11 a.m. on Sunday may still be the most segregated hour of the Southern week—but this is much more the result of different religious traditions and styles than a last vestige of segregation. Electronic preachers—even the discredited Jim Bakker and Jimmy Swaggart—have or had their integrated live congregations, while the South's most famous evangelist, Billy Graham, frequently shares the pulpit or the podium with black ministers. "Hamburger integration" it may have been, but the provision of equal access to public accommodations has removed the most obvious and humiliating symbol of the Southern caste system.

The burgeoning black middle class has been best able to take advantage of these changes, from dining in elegant restaurants to competing for lucrative executive and professional positions. David Goldfield has called the growth of the

Southern black middle class in the 1980s the "major economic story of the decade." Certainly the statistics are impressive. By the mid-1980s 30 percent of Southern black workers held middle-class jobs, compared to 4 percent in 1940. For blacks able to take advantage of vastly increased access to higher education, legislative provisions against job discrimination, and affirmative-action policies put in place by federal and state governments in the 1970s, the South was now a frontier of opportunity.

One striking result was the reversal of the migration pattern. For almost a century blacks had left the South whenever it was possible to do so, for the relatively freer existence and expanded employment opportunities offered by the cities of the Northeast and Midwest. Since 1975 this trend has been reversed: the numbers of blacks moving South has persistently exceeded those leaving. Some are former Southerners returning home, others are seeing the region for the first time, drawn by the promise of expanding economic horizons and a more relaxed, less racially influenced lifestyle. Most are professionals, with degrees and diplomas aplenty. Already living middle-class lives, they have greatly expanded the Southern black middle-class base. Almost all have stayed. Those returning home after years away find the change in the racial climate remarkable, and much less abrasive than in New York or Chicago. First-time Southerners feel the same. Colin Batson, a New Yorker who moved to Charlotte in 1985, reinforces the point: "I was scared about what would come to me down here," he said, but his experience had been overwhelmingly positive. "I'm sorry I didn't move here ten years ago. . . . I've found that a lot of people treat you nicer than they do in New York. . . . Quite honestly, I haven't come across anything I don't like about the South." Of course, most of these immigrants went to the cities. The small towns of the South have changed much less dramatically. Nevertheless it must be emphasized that the emergence of an affluent, well-educated, and politically sophisticated black middle class has been the most significant feature of Southern life over the past two decades, and that the civil rights movement made it happen. Its very presence means that, regardless of the twists and turns of race relations in the future, there can be no going back to the segregated past—except in the minds of some obscurantist whites.

There are, however, two black communities in the South, just as there are in New York, Cleveland, or Chicago. As the black middle class grew in confidence and affluence in the 1980s, so the gulf between it and black "have nots" widened. Atlanta, the South's largest city, where political power is well entrenched, has a core area with poverty levels almost as drastic as Newark or Detroit, while black political control of many of the region's rural counties has not erased the hopelessness and deprivation found within them. The publicity surrounding the 1968 Poor People's Campaign first revealed to the nation the shocking depths of Southern rural poverty; this has not changed, and the South's rural poor are disproportionately black. Social workers, government surveys, welfare reformers, and journalists all have painted horrifying pictures of deprivation and degradation in the rural South; of people too ignorant even to be aware of the most basic services available to them; of dietary, sanitary, educational, and employment deficiencies that match in every way those uncovered during the Great Depression. Those worse off, in increasing proportion, are women and children. Welfare services, reduced over the past decades, cannot provide more than palliative care. Southern rural poverty remains as it always has been, a reproach to basic American standards of decency.

In Southern cities, too, there is poverty amidst the boosterism and growth. Again it is disproportionately black, exacerbated by another type of migration, that of the rural poor to the city slums. The journalist Neal Pierce wrote in 1980 that "black slums in Atlanta, New Orleans, Birmingham, Richmond and Jackson . . . were among the most despair ridden in America." Ironically all five cities at the time had black mayors. Thus access to power does not necessarily bring socioeconomic change, only heightened expectations. The so-called black underclass, its emergence and intractability so much a concern for welfare workers, journalists, and social commentators in the past decade, is not only a phenomenon of the Northern ghettos. Southern urban poverty is every bit as urgent, and the solutions every bit as elusive. The civil rights revolution, while it opened a world of opportunity to Southern blacks, did not provide all of them with the means to enter it.

The civil rights revolution had its roots deep in the American experience, in the egalitarian notions of Thomas Jefferson, the Emancipation Proclamation, the writings of Frederick Douglass and Sojourner Truth. It is a mistake to think that Southern blacks meekly accepted the imposition of a caste system. They fought against it from the beginning, as they had previously resisted slavery, and this despite the power massed on the other side. Gradually they won small victories, long before civil rights became a national issue. Nevertheless, the years between 1955 and 1968 saw the movement at its zenith, and it transformed the South and cleansed the nation of a great moral evil. Many men and women contributed to the triumph—Charles Houston and his lawyers; the returning veterans of World War II; Charles DeLaine; Mose Wright; Jo Ann Robinson and her Women's Political Council; the nine children of Little Rock; James Meredith; the Freedom Riders; the brave young men and women of SNCC; Fanny Lou

Hamer; John Lewis; even Stokely Carmichael. But it was Martin Luther King who became the movement's embodiment, who gave it its ideology, whose words and actions best demonstrated its moral purpose. Let King, therefore, have the last word. In Montgomery, at the start of it all, in his very first speech to a mass audience, he expressed the fervent hope that

> When the history books are written in the future, somebody will have to say, "There lived a race of people—a black people—a people who had the marvelous courage to stand up for their rights, and thereby they injected a new meaning into the veins of history and of civilization." And we are going to do that. God grant that we will do it, before it is too late.

Martin Luther King, and the people he led, fulfilled this hope.

A Note on Sources

IN WRITING A brief history of the civil rights movement, one is conscious of traversing familiar ground. In particular I relied on three superb surveys of the movement, each differing slightly in perspective. These were Harvard Sitkoff's brilliant *The Struggle for Black Equality, 1954–1980* (New York, 1981), David Goldfield's *Black, White, and Southern: Race Relations and Southern Culture, 1940 to the Present* (Baton Rouge, 1990), and Manning Marable's *Race, Reform and Rebellion: The Second Reconstruction in Black America, 1945–1982* (Jackson, Miss., 1984). My debt to these scholars is obvious and easily recognizable from the frequency with which they are quoted. I have also used extensively Allen Matusow's *The Unravelling of America: A History of Liberalism in the 1960s* (New York, 1984), easily the best overview of the 1960s. For a superb study of the whole postwar era, see William H. Chafe, *The Unfinished Journey: America Since World War II* (New York, 1995).

The classic study of the legal challenge to school segregation, which climaxed in the *Brown* decision, is Richard Kluger, *Simple Justice: The History of Brown v. Board of Education and Black America's Struggle for Equality* (New York, 1976). John Egerton's magisterial *Speak Now Against the Day: The Generation Before the Civil Rights Movement in the South* (New York, 1994) was indispensable for the pre-1945 years, supplemented by Anthony Dunbar, *Against the Grain: Southern Radicals and Prophets, 1929–1959* (Charlottesville, Va., 1981); Morton Sosna, *In Search of the Silent South: Southern Liberals and the Race Issue* (New York, 1977); Robin Kelley, *Hammer and Hoe: Alabama Communists During the Great Depression* (Chapel Hill, 1990); and my own biographies of Southern liberals, *A Southern Rebel: The Life and Times of Aubrey*

Willis Williams, 1890–1965 (Chapel Hill, 1983), *Miss Lucy of the CIO: The Life and Times of Lucy Randolph Mason, 1882–1959* (Athens, Ga., 1988), and *The Conscience of a Lawyer: Clifford J. Durr and American Civil Liberties, 1899–1975* (Tuscaloosa, Ala., 1990). I also used Robert F. Martin's excellent article "Critique of Southern Society and Vision of a New Order: The Fellowship of Southern Churchmen, 1934–1957," *Church History*, vol. 52 (March 1983). For the New Deal era see Harvard Sitkoff, *A New Deal for Blacks: The Emergence of Civil Rights as a National Issue* (New York, 1978).

My account of the crises at the University of Alabama is drawn principally from E. Culpepper Clark, *The Schoolhouse Door: Segregation's Last Stand at the University of Alabama* (New York, 1993); that at Central High is from Elizabeth Huckaby, *Crisis at Central High: Little Rock, 1957–58* (Baton Rouge, 1980). The integration of Ole Miss is fully discussed in John Dittmer, *Local People: The Struggle for Civil Rights in Mississippi* (Urbana, Ill., 1994), one of three superb state and local studies I used frequently. The other two were Adam Fairclough, *Race and Democracy: The Civil Rights Struggle in Louisiana, 1915–1972* (Athens, Ga., 1995) and William Chafe, *Civilities and Civil Rights: Greensboro, North Carolina, and the Black Struggle for Freedom* (New York, 1980).

Scholarship on the life and work of Martin Luther King is extensive. The best short biography is Adam Fairclough, *Martin Luther King, Jr.* (Athens, Ga., 1995). Longer studies that I used frequently were David Garrow, *Bearing the Cross: Martin Luther King, Jr. and the Southern Christian Leadership Conference* (New York, 1986); Adam Fairclough, *To Redeem the Soul of America: The Southern Christian Leadership Conference and Martin Luther King, Jr.* (Athens, Ga., 1987); and Taylor Branch, *Parting the Waters: America in the King Years, 1954–63* (New York, 1988). For the Montgomery boycott I also used Henry Bedford's excellent chapter in *Trouble Downtown: The Local Context of Twentieth-Century America* (New York, 1978). On the SNCC, see Clayborne Carson,

In Struggle: SNCC and the Black Awakening of the 1960s (Cambridge, Mass., 1981). My discussion of white resistance is drawn mainly from Numan V. Bartley, *The Rise of Massive Resistance: Race and Politics in the South During the 1950s* (Baton Rouge, 1969) and Neil R. McMillen, *The Citizens' Council: Organized Resistance to the Second Reconstruction, 1954–64* (Urbana, Ill., 1971). On the federal judges who were crucial in supporting civil rights litigants, see Jack Bass, *Unlikely Heroes: The Southern Judges Who Made the Civil Rights Revolution* (New York, 1981) and Tinsley E. Yarbrough, *Judge Frank Johnson and Human Rights in Alabama* (Tuscaloosa, Ala., 1984).

For the evolution and implementation of federal government civil rights policy, I chiefly used Robert F. Burk, *The Eisenhower Administration and Black Civil Rights* (Knoxville, Tenn., 1984); Carl M. Brauer, *John F. Kennedy and the Second Reconstruction* (Cambridge, Mass., 1977); and Hugh D. Graham, *The Civil Rights Era: Origins and Development of National Policy, 1960–1972* (New York, 1990). I also used the excellent chapter in James N. Giglio, *The Presidency of John F. Kennedy* (Lawrence, Kans., 1991). For the voting rights campaign, see David Garrow, *Protest at Selma: Martin Luther King, Jr., and the Voting Rights Act of 1965* (New Haven, 1978). For the act's effect, see Steven F. Lawson, *Black Ballots: Voting Rights in the South, 1944–1969* (New York, 1976) and *In Pursuit of Power: Southern Blacks and Electoral Politics, 1965–1982* (New York, 1985). See also Alexander P. Lamis, *The Two-Party South* (New York, 1984) and Carl Abbott, *The New Urban America: Growth and Politics in Sunbelt Cities* (Chapel Hill, 1981). For school desegregation, see Frye Gaillard, *The Dream Long Deferred* (Chapel Hill, 1988).

Finally, my understanding of the events of these years has been deepened by the reading of many firsthand accounts, the memoirs of the participants, sometimes collected and anthologized, sometimes published singly. I cannot possibly list all of them here, but those I have drawn on most frequently, not only for this work but for my teaching and general understanding over the years, include Howell Raines, *My Soul Is Rested: Movement Days in the Deep South Remembered* (New York, 1977); Martin Luther King, Jr., *Stride Toward Freedom: The Montgomery Story* (New York, 1958); Hollinger F. Barnard, ed., *Outside the Magic Circle: The Autobiography of Virginia Foster Durr* (Tuscaloosa, Ala., 1985); Anne Moody, *Coming of Age in Mississippi* (New York, 1968); Sally Belfrage, *Freedom Summer* (New York, 1965); and Theodore Rosengarten, *All God's Dangers: The Life of Nate Shaw* (New York, 1974). Those interested in the movement are also referred to the superb PBS television documentary series *Eyes on the Prize: America's Civil Rights Years* (New York, 1987). The account of Wilson Head's journey was found in the papers of the NAACP in the Library of Congress.

Unfortunately I had completed the manuscript before the availability to me of three excellent new books, each of which add valuable insights to what has been written here. They are Numan Bartley's final volume in the History of the South series, *The New South, 1945–1980* (Baton Rouge, 1995); James Patterson's volume in the Oxford History of the United States, *Grand Expectations: Postwar America, 1945–1974* (New York, 1996); and Patricia Sullivan's study of the early civil rights years, *Days of Hope: Race and Democracy in the New Deal Era* (Chapel Hill, 1996).

Index

Abernathy, Ralph, 54, 91; and Albany campaign, 69–71; becomes SCLC secretary, 64; and Birmingham, 74; and Selma campaign, 130; and Washington march, 79
Alabama Sharecroppers Union (ASU), 14–15
Alabama, University of, and desegregation, 32–34, 46–49, 155
Albany, Ga., campaign, 68–72; failure of, 72–77; and Kennedys, 112–113
Almond, J. Lindsay, 39
American Federation of Labor (AFL), 16
Azbell, Joe, 54

Baker, Ella, 65–66, 87
Barnett, Ross, 42–44, 46, 113–114
Bevel, James, 140, 145
Birmingham, Ala., campaign: campaign opens, 73–74; and "children's" crusade, 75–76; importance of, 77; and negotiations, 76–77; reasons for, 72–73; and violence, 76
Black Caucus (congressional), 150–151
Black, Hugo, 11
Black Panther party, 137
Bond, Julian, 67; leads "sit-in," 85–86
Brown, Minnijean, 37–38
Brown v. Board of Education, 8–9, 81; arguments heard, 24–25; compliance urged, 27–28; evasion of, 40–41; implementation of, 29, 50; importance of, 25–26, 155–156; and Mississippi, 45; opposition to, 27, 29–31, 34–35, 106
Byrd, Harry F., 27

Carmichael, Stokely: becomes SNCC president, 137; and "black power," 137–139; importance of, 163
Carter, Jimmy, 149–150, 154
Chafe, William, 39, 81
Chaney, James, 103–104, 153

Civil Rights Act of 1964: effect of, 83, 120–121, 125, 134–135, 159; King's influence on, 80; main features of, 115–116; opposition to, 116, 119; passage of, 117–120; proposed, 78, 115; Republican support for, 117–120. *See also* Civil rights legislation.
Civil rights legislation: 1957 act passed, 107–108; passage of 1964 act, 117–120; 1968 act passed, 147
Civil War, ix–x
Clark, Jim, 128–130, 141
Clinton, Bill, 154
Communist Party of the United States (CPUSA), 14–15
Congress of Industrial Organizations (CIO), 11–12, 16–18
Congress of Racial Equality (CORE), 77, 116; and Freedom Rides, 88–91; importance of, 92; philosophy of, 88; and voter registration, 95–97
Connor, Eugene ("Bull"), 73, 75–77, 141
Daley, Richard J., 140–142
DeLaine, J. A., 8, 162
Demographic change, 18, 160–161
Dennis, David, 102–104
Dirksen, Everett B., 117, 120
Dittmer, John, 20, 29, 41
Doar, John, 43
Douglass, Frederick, 4
Du Bois, W. E. B., 4
Durr, Clifford, J., 10,12, 52
Durr, Virginia F., 52, 59

Eastland, James O., 27, 33, 35, 78, 92
Egerton, John, 15
Eisenhower, Dwight D., 24, 43, 109; and *Brown* decision, 29–30, 34, 106; and civil rights legislation, 107–108; and Little Rock crisis, 36–38; and segregation, 106–107
Evers, Medgar, 20–22, 42, 115

Fairclough, Adam, 95
Farmer, James, 77, 79; and Freedom Rides, 88–90, 92; supports MFDP compromise, 124; and voter registration, 96
Faubus, Orval, 34–39, 43, 107, 153

Fellowship of Southern Churchmen (FSC), 13
Folsom, James M., 19, 27
Forman, James, 94, 136
Franklin, John Hope, 24
Freedom Ride movement, 3, 87–92; importance of, 92–93, 162; violence toward, 89–92
Freedom Summer project, activities of, 103–104; and MFDP, 104–105; origins of, 102; and racial tensions, 136–137; workers murdered, 102–104. *See also* Mississippi Freedom Democratic Party.

Gaines v. Canada, 5–6
Ghetto riots, 138–139, 146
Gingrich, Newt, 153
Goldfield, David, 30, 38, 50, 153, 159–160
Goldwater, Barry, 122, 125
Goodman, Andrew, 103–104, 153
Gray, Fred, 53, 59

Halleck, Charles B., 117
Hamer, Fannie Lou: honored on death, 153; legacy of, 162–163; rejects MFDP compromise, 124; speech at 1964 convention, 123; and voter registration, 98–99
Head, Wilson A., 3–4, 87, 149
Henry, Aaron, 21–22
Herndon, Angelo, 15
Highlander Folk School, 15–16, 52, 66
Hodges, Luther B., 40
Hood, James A., 47
Horton, Myles, 15–16
Houston, Charles H., 4–5; legacy of, 9, 162
Howard University, 4–5
Humphrey, Hubert H., 123–124

Johnson, Frank, 131–132
Johnson, Lyndon B., 11, 103, 108, 113, 145–146; dislike of King, 127; federalizes Alabama guard, 133; and Great Society, 127, 140; and 1964 Civil Rights Act, 118–120; and 1964 election, 122–125; proposes fair-housing legislation, 142; and voting rights bill, 129, 132
Jordan, Barbara, 150

Katzenbach, Nicholas, 48
Kennedy, John F., 38; and Albany crisis, 112–113;

Kennedy, John F. (*cont.*): assassination of, 117–118; assumes national leadership, 114–116; cautious approach of, 111–112; federalizes Alabama Guard, 48–49; and Freedom Rides, 91–92; and 1960 election, 109; and Ole Miss crisis, 41–45, 113–114; opposes Washington march, 78–79, 117; proposes civil rights bill, 77–78, 115; telephones Mrs. King, 67; views on civil rights, 108–110, 114

Kennedy, Robert F.: announces presidential bid, 145; assassination of, 147; and Freedom Rides, 90–92; and King's death, 146–147; and 1964 act, 120; and Ole Miss crisis, 41–45; secures King's release, 67; and SNCC, 111–112; views on civil rights, 116–117; and voter registration, 94, 96, 111; and voting rights violations, 110–111

Kester, Howard, 13–14

King, Coretta Scott: background of, 56–57; and John F. Kennedy, 67; and 1976 Democratic convention, 149–150

King, Lonnie, 85–86

King, Martin Luther, Jr., 32, 52; and Albany campaign, 67–71; assassination of, 146; background of, 55–56; becomes national figure, 61–62, 80; beliefs of, 56, 63–64, 143–144; and Birmingham success, 77; and "black power," 138–139; Chicago campaign fails, 140–142; effect of death, 146–147; and Freedom Rides, 91–93; forms SCLC, 64–65; and Gandhi, 56, 63; "I Have a Dream" speech of, 79–80; invited to Birmingham, 73–74; jailed in Atlanta, 67; and John F. Kennedy, 110; leads Montgomery Bus Boycott, 54–55, 58–60; leads march to Montgomery, 129–130, 132–133; legacy of, 148, 163; and "Letter from the Birmingham Jail," 74; loses prestige, 72; makes secret deal, 131–132, 135; and Malcolm X, 100–101; and Memphis garbage strike, 145–146; moves to Atlanta, 66; moves SCLC north, 140; moves toward socialism, 144; and 1964 Civil Rights Act,

116; wins Nobel Prize, 127; and nonviolence, 63–64, 80, 138; opposes Vietnam War, 143; plans Poor People's Campaign, 144–145; proposes Washington march, 78; relations with Lyndon Johnson, 127; and segregation, 57–58, 74–75, 79–80; Selma campaign of, 128–132; and "sit-ins," 82–83, 87; and SNCC, 97–98; supports MFDP compromise, 124
King, Martin Luther, Sr. ("Daddy"), 53, 67
Ku Klux Klan, 31, 103–104; diminished influence of, 158–159; humiliation of, 61–62

Lawson, James, 87
Levinson, Stanley, 66
Lewis, John, 89–90, 129–130, 150, 163
Little Rock, Ark., 34–38
Lowenstein, Allard, 13, 99
Lucy, Autherine, 32–33, 46, 107

Maddox, Lester, 121
Malcolm X, 73, 75; contempt for King, 101; militant views of, 100–101, 138; and Southern blacks, 101–102
Malone, Vivian, 46–47
Marshall, Thurgood, 5–7, 110; and Autherine Lucy, 33; and *Briggs v. Eliot,* 8; and *Brown* decision, 8–9, 24–25
Martin, Robert F., 13
Mason, Lucy Randolph, 10, 12, 17
Matusow, Allen, 120, 129, 133–134
McCulloch, William M., 117
McLaurin v. Oklahoma, 6–7
Meredith, James H., 41–45, 75, 113–114, 138, 151, 162
Mississippi Freedom Democratic Party (MFDP), formation of, 104–105; and 1964 Democratic convention, 122–123, 127; rejects compromise, 124
Mississippi, University of (Ole Miss), 41–45, 155
Mitchell, H. L., 13–14
Montgomery Bus Boycott, 16, 83; begins, 53–54; failure to settle, 57–58; gains national attention, 60; significance of, 61–62, 153
Montgomery Improvement Association (MIA): and the community, 58; indicted,

Montgomery Improvement Association (*cont.*): 60–61; and negotiations, 57; organization of, 54–55
Moody, Anne, 23
Moore, Amzie, 95
Morton, Nelle, 13
Moses, Robert: and Freedom Summer, 99–102; and MFDP, 105; and voter registration, 95–97
Motley, Constance Baker, 42

Nash, Diane, 85
National Association for the Advancement of Colored People (NAACP), 4–6; and Albany project, 68–70; and *Brown* decision, 24–25, 31; and CORE, 88, 93; and Greensboro, N.C., 40–41; and John F. Kennedy, 109; and Little Rock, 34–35; and Montgomery Bus Boycott, 52–53; and Mississippi, 21, 29; and Ole Miss, 42; outlawed in Alabama, 60; and SCLC, 64, 99; and SNCC, 99–100; and University of Alabama, 32–33, 47; and white primary, 12
New Deal, 9–11, 16–17
Nixon, E. D., 52–53
Nixon, Richard M., 107–109

Parks, Rosa, 16, 59; arrest of, 51–53; conviction of, 54
Patterson, John, 46, 91
Plessy v. Ferguson, 7, 24–25
Poverty, Southern, 10, 144, 161–162
Price, Cecil, 103–104, 153
Pritchett, Laurie, 68–69, 71–73, 112–113

Rainey, Laurence, 103
Randolph, A. Philip, 78–79
Reconstruction, x, 94, 116
Republican party, 153
Robinson, Jo Ann, 53, 162
Roosevelt, Eleanor, 10–11
Roosevelt, Franklin D., 9–10
Russell, Richard, 108, 119
Rustin, Bayard, 63, 125; influence on King, 66; and MFDP compromise, 124; and 1947 Freedom Ride, 88

Schwerner, Michael, 102–104, 153
Scottsboro boys, 15
Segregation, racial: black resistance to, x–xi, 3–4; and

bus boycott, 57–58, 61; defense of, 31, 35, 38, 57, 59–60, 73; King's critique of, 74–75, 79–80; legal challenges to, 6–9; origins of, ix–xi; residential segregation, 156–157; school segregation ends, 134–135, 155–157
Selma, Ala, campaign, 128–129; gains national attention, 130–132; success of, 133–134; violence of, 130–131
Sherrod, Charles, 68–69
Shuttlesworth, Fred, 32, 73, 90
"Sit-in" movement: beginning of, 81–82; movement spreads, 83–85; significance of, 86–87; tactics of, 84; violence toward, 84–85
Sitkoff, Harvard, 62, 124–125
Smith, Howard K., 119
Smith, Lillian, 12
Smith v. Allwright, 12
Southern Christian Leadership Conference (SCLC): and Birmingham campaign, 73, 76–77; challenges to, 93; and Chicago campaign, 140–141; chooses Selma,128–129; early years of, 64–66; formation of, 64; invited to Albany, 69; leaves Albany, 72; and Poor People's Campaign, 145; and "sit-ins," 82, 87; SNCC contempt for, 135. *See also* King, Martin Luther, Jr.
Southern Conference for Human Welfare (SCHW), 11–13, 16–17, 52
Southern Manifesto, 31
Southern Regional Council, 13
Southern Tenant Farmers Union (STFU), 13–14
Stennis, John, 28, 153
Student Nonviolent Coordinating Committee (SNCC): and Albany project, 68–69; breaks with King, 124, 132, 135–136; breaks with liberals, 124–125, 135; creation of, 66–67, 87; differences with SCLC, 72, 136; distrust of Kennedys, 111, 116; and Freedom Rides, 90–92; legacy of, 162; and local people, 98–99; and rage, 136; and Selma campaign, 131–132; and separatism, 137–139, 145; sexual tensions within, 136; supports MFDP, 124; violence toward, 96–97, 99, 136; and voter registration, 94–96; and white students, 99–100, 136–137

Supreme Court, U.S., 6–7; and *Brown* decision, 23–26; and implementation of *Brown,* 31; and interstate travel, 3, 61; and redistricting, 150–151; and school desegregation, 155–156

Talmadge, Herman, 27
Thurmond, Strom, 153
Till, Emmett: effect of trial, 23; lynching of, 22–23, 159
Truman, Harry S., 13, 19–20, 106

Voting behavior (of blacks): and local politics, 152; and Mississippi, 41; and 1964 election, 125–128; and 1965 Voting Rights Act, 133–134, 151–152, 154; and World War II, 18–21

Walker, Wyatt T., 66, 69, 77
Wallace, George C.: bans Selma-Montgomery march, 130; campaigns for president, 121–122; refuses to protect marchers, 132; repudiates segregationist views, 149–150, 152–153; and University of Alabama, 46–49; views on segregation, 46
Wallace, Henry, 12–13
Waring, J. Waties, 8, 21
Warren, Earl, 24–25, 29, 106
West, Ben, 85
White Citizens Council: and Montgomery Bus Boycott, 59; and Mississippi, 41; rise of, 30; tactics of, 31, 46; and University of Alabama, 33
Wilder, Douglas, 151–152
Wilkins, Roy, 79, 109, 116, 124
Williams, Aubrey, 9–11, 52
Williams, Hosea, 130
Woodward, C. Vann, ix–x, 24
Wright, Mose, 22–23, 162

Young, Andrew, 113, 120, 132, 150

Zellner, Robert, 137

A NOTE ON THE AUTHOR

John A. Salmond is professor of American history at La Trobe University in Melbourne, Australia. Born in New Zealand, he studied at the University of Otago in New Zealand and received a Ph.D. from Duke University. He has been a Fulbright Scholar and a recipient of awards from the American Council of Learned Societies, the Eleanor Roosevelt Foundation, and the Gustavus Myers Foundation, and has also written *Gastonia, 1929; The Conscience of a Lawyer; Miss Lucy of the CIO; A Southern Rebel;* and *The Civilian Conservation Corps.* He lives in Victoria, Australia.

BOOKS IN THE AMERICAN WAYS SERIES

William Earl Weeks, *Building the Continental Empire: American Expansion from the Revolution to the Civil War*

Jean V. Matthews, *Women's Struggle for Equality: The First Phase, 1820–1876*

Curtis D. Johnson, *Redeeming America: Evangelicals and the Road to Civil War*

J. Matthew Gallman, *The North Fights the Civil War: The Home Front*

Maury Klein, *The Flowering of the Third America: The Making of an Organizational Society, 1850–1920*

Larry M. Logue, *To Appomattox and Beyond: The Civil War Soldier in War and Peace*

Robert Muccigrosso, *Celebrating the New World: Chicago's Columbian Exposition of 1893*

Daniel Nelson, *Shifting Fortunes: The Rise and Decline of American Labor, from the 1820s to the Present*

Thomas R. Pegram, *Battling Demon Rum: The Struggle for a Dry America, 1800–1933*

Roger Daniels, *Not Like Us: Immigrants and Minorities in America, 1890–1924*

Burton W. Peretti, *Jazz in American Culture*

Iwan W. Morgan, *Deficit Government: Taxing and Spending in Modern America*

D. Clayton James and Anne Sharp Wells, *From Pearl Harbor to V-J Day: The American Armed Forces in World War II*

John W. Jeffries, *Wartime America: The World War II Home Front*

John Earl Haynes, *Red Scare or Red Menace?: American Communism and Anticommunism in the Cold War Era*

Mark J. White, *Missiles in Cuba: Kennedy, Khrushchev, Castro and the 1962 Crisis*

John A. Salmond, *"My Mind Set on Freedom": A History of the Civil Rights Movement, 1954–1968*

John A. Andrew III, *Lyndon Johnson and the Great Society*

Lewis L. Gould, *1968: The Election That Changed America*